About the Authors

Michael Mazzeo is an associate professor of management and strategy at Northwestern University's Kellogg School of Management, where he teaches the school's core MBA class in business strategy. Mike has a PhD in economics from Stanford University and lives in Chicago with his ten-year-old son and many, many Legos.

Paul Oyer is the Fred H. Merrill Professor of Economics at Stanford University's Graduate School of Business. Paul has a PhD in economics from Princeton University and lives in Stanford, California with his two children.

Scott Schaefer holds the Kendall D. Garff Chair in Business Administration and is professor of finance at the University of Utah's David Eccles School of Business. He has a PhD in business economics from Stanford University's Graduate School of Business and lives in Salt Lake City with his two children.

The Roadside MBA

Real-world Lessons for Entrepreneurs,
Start-ups and Small Businesses

Michael Mazzeo

Paul Oyer

Scott Schaefer

PAN BOOKS

First published 2014 in the US as *Roadside MBA* by
Business Plus, an imprint of Grand Central Publishing

First published in the UK 2014 by Macmillan

This paperback edition published 2015 by Pan Books
an imprint of Pan Macmillan, a division of Macmillan Publishers Limited
Pan Macmillan, 20 New Wharf Road, London N1 9RR
Basingstoke and Oxford
Associated companies throughout the world
www.panmacmillan.com

ISBN 978-1-4472-8633-2

Book design by Carin Dow

1 3 5 7 9 8 6 4 2

A CIP catalogue record for this book is available from the British Library.

Printed and bound by CPI Group (UK) Ltd, Croydon, CR0 4YY

Visit **www.panmacmillan.com** to read more about all our books
and to buy them. You will also find features, author interviews and
news of any author events, and you can sign up for e-newsletters
so that you're always first to hear about our new releases.

To Charlie—MM
To David and Lucy—PO
To Curtis and Rosie—SS
Hope you liked the T-shirts from the road.

Contents

The Roadside MBA

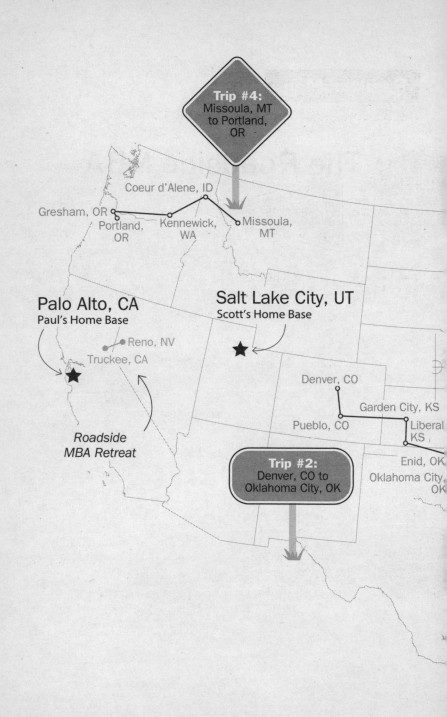

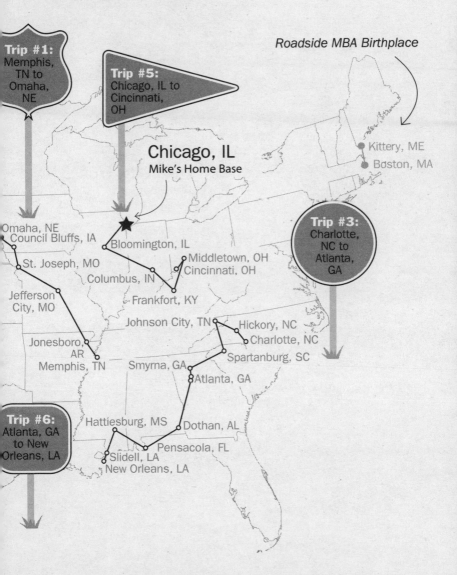

Ramblin' Men

The Six Voyages of The Roadside MBA

Trip #1:
Memphis, TN to Omaha, NE

Trip #5:
Chicago, IL to Cincinnati, OH

Roadside MBA Birthplace

Kittery, ME
Boston, MA

Chicago, IL
Mike's Home Base

Omaha, NE
Council Bluffs, IA
St. Joseph, MO
Bloomington, IL
Middletown, OH
Cincinnati, OH
Columbus, IN
Jefferson City, MO
Frankfort, KY
Johnson City, TN
Hickory, NC
Charlotte, NC
Jonesboro, AR
Memphis, TN
Smyrna, GA
Spartanburg, SC
Atlanta, GA
Hattiesburg, MS
Dothan, AL
Pensacola, FL
Slidell, LA
New Orleans, LA

Trip #3:
Charlotte, NC to Atlanta, GA

Trip #6:
Atlanta, GA to New Orleans, LA

Prologue

LIGHTHEARTED (AND IN SEARCH OF FOOTWEAR), WE TAKE TO THE OPEN ROAD

After an economics conference in Boston, the three of us—all business professors—had a bit of time to kill before our flights home, so we decided to hit the road. Mike had never set foot in Maine, so for kicks we drove an hour north on I-95, stopping for a wicked good lunch at Bob's Clam Hut just over the state line. Figuring a walk might help us digest our deep-fried seafood, we wandered into a shoe store just across from the restaurant. We weren't looking to buy shoes, but the sales staff insisted on asking us repeatedly whether we might want to try something on. Scott, who likes his solitude, asked a salesman why he was being so insistent even after having been told "no, thanks" a couple of times. The salesman, later joined by the manager and all of the rest of the store's employees, proceeded to describe in amazing detail the store owner's "secret shopper" program, in which employees can be marked down if they are not sufficiently persistent when working with customers. Paul and Mike soon wandered over, and the three of us began asking the shoe store's team all sorts of questions about topics we teach to MBA students—sales incentives, relationships with suppliers, product differentiation, and competition. It was twice as educational as the conference we had just attended, and the conversation extended so long that we had to exceed the speed limit to get back to Boston for our flights. This chance conversation allowed a sneak peek into the workings of a small establishment, and, to us, it was thoroughly exhilarating.

We are economists and professors who have been teaching business strategy classes to MBA students for years. Paul Oyer, a professor at Stanford, is slim with thinning blond hair and could—in the movie version of our lives—be played by Police front man Sting, perhaps with makeup to make him a bit Jewish-looking. The oldest member of our group, Paul spent a few years in the so-called real world before starting work on his economics PhD, and he is also most likely to tell, and perhaps retell, a joke that isn't very funny.

Scott Schaefer, a professor at the University of Utah, is not quite short but definitely not tall and has a full head of brown hair; imagine a casting of Jason Alexander (George from *Seinfeld*) in a bushy wig. Scott fancies himself a lovable curmudgeon, which Mike and Paul agree is about half right.

Mike Mazzeo, bespectacled with close-cropped hair and a quick sense of humor, is a professor at Northwestern University. Mike is the youngest and most impressionable of our group and has yet to meet a fad diet he was unwilling to try. As far as Paul and Scott can tell, Mike's only character flaw is a lifelong devotion to the New York Yankees; think Ben Stiller with a Derek Jeter complex.

We all started our professorial careers at Northwestern University's Kellogg School of Management; Scott arrived in 1995 after completing a PhD at Stanford, Paul a year later from Princeton, and Mike from Stanford in 1998. Finding many shared interests—baseball, beer, dogs (canines, not frankfurters), and, of course, economics—we became friends through our publish-or-perish days as assistant professors, and remained close even after Paul left for California in 2000 and Scott for Utah in 2005.

Over the years, we've taught thousands of MBAs at leading business schools. A majority of our students have gone on to work for (or consult with) large companies, so our classes have tended to focus on strategic issues facing big business. We've taught cases about Intel, Southwest Airlines, Procter & Gamble, Nordstrom...the list is pretty long.

Our unplanned visit to a Maine shoe store made us realize that the strategic challenges that small businesses face are just as rich and compelling as anything being discussed inside Six Sigma redoubts like General Electric. And the knife cuts both ways: the MBA tactics and tenets we teach would, we think, be just as valuable in the hands of a small business owner as they are in the hands of a Kraft brand manager or a Bain consultant.

To us, this meant just one thing...

Road Trip!

Fast-forward a year: Mike's and Paul's marriages had just ended, and Scott's—unbeknownst to him at the time—wasn't going well.

"Hey guys, I have an idea I want to bounce off you," Scott began the conference call. "Remember last December, when we went to that shoe store in Maine?"

"How could I forget? I learned more there than I did in five years of graduate school," said Mike, always the quipper.

"I keep wishing I could go back and get data on their compensation plans," Paul added. (And yes, this is exactly the sort of thing economists lie awake at night thinking about.) "I probably discussed five examples from that shoe store when I was teaching a Strategic Human Resources Management course this year."

"I know, I can't stop thinking about it either," Scott said, with a passion he normally reserves for occasional anti-Yankee diatribes. "Suppose we try to do that again, and again, and again. How do you think your courses would be different if you had examples from ten or fifteen businesses like that?"

"That could be interesting," Mike said, "but we only see each other at conferences once or twice a year."

"Right," Scott said. "So we take a road trip, just for this. Suppose we find a week this summer where neither of you has your kids and hit the road in search of interesting small businesses?"

"This is either the best idea you've ever had, or the worst," Paul commented. "I'm not sure which. How do you think we'll find interesting businesses, and how do we get them to talk to us about strategic challenges?"

"Well, I'm not exactly sure," Scott admitted. "But look at it this way—if the businesses are boring or we can't get people to open up, at least you get a road trip out of the deal. What states haven't you been to?"

Paul religiously tracks which states he's visited (which a lot of people do) and also states where he's spent the night (which is a little weird). "I've never spent the night in Missouri or North Dakota."

"Missouri it is," Scott asserted, having spent a few too many uncomfortable nights on the couches of his North Dakota extended family.

"Guys, there might be a book to be written here," Mike interjected. "We collect examples from the road of interesting strategic problems facing small businesses, then show how the frameworks we teach in our MBA classes apply. I bet the average small business owner could really benefit from a dose of strategic reasoning; it'd be a great introduction for business owners who haven't done an MBA, and a solid refresher for those who have."

"Like *Economics of Strategy*, but applied to small business?" Scott said, shamelessly plugging the textbook he co-authored.

"Uhhhh, sure," said Mike, "but maybe not so heavy on the math?"

"We'll call it *The Roadside MBA*!" Paul exclaimed.

"OK, I'll check about taking a week away from my family this summer, and you guys check your parenting schedules. Compare notes in a week?" Scott said.

"Sounds good," Mike responded.

"If we take US Highway 59, we can go from Missouri *to* Dakota!" Paul exclaimed, glancing up from Google Maps.

"You're on your own for North Dakota, pal," Scott replied.

And our project was born.

What Do Three Egghead Economists Know About Running a Business, Anyway?

Why, given our backgrounds as economics PhDs, would leading business schools ask us to teach classes on strategy? Isn't economics all that stuff about money supply and inflation and where the stock market is going? And what does that have to do with business strategy?

We three are what's known in the trade as micro-economists. We get down in the nitty-gritty. We don't forecast economic growth or future unemployment trends; instead, we apply economic reasoning to the study of companies, individuals, and markets. Mike's PhD dissertation, a data-driven study of how rural interstate motels differentiate themselves from local competition, grew out of his own on-the-road observations when driving from New York State to California to begin graduate school. Paul's thesis on how quota-based employee compensation plans contribute to the seasonality of corporate earnings stemmed from his post-college jobs at 3Com and Booz Allen. While working in the real world, he was often frustrated with co-workers and clients who were more focused on quarterly targets than on long-term value. And Scott's dissertation, which examined the forces that make organizational change so difficult, foreshadowed his own later attempts to re-engineer the University of Utah's School of Business while serving as associate dean. With just those three topics—one study of how companies compete in product markets, one looking at how companies structure pay for employees, and another of how companies can organize for success—we've covered much of what keeps business people up at night.

Our years of applying economic reasoning to strategic questions have led us to a pretty simple philosophy of business strategy, one that Mike has so repeatedly emphasized in his classes that we named it after him.

> **Mazzeo's Law**
> The answer to every strategic question is
> "It depends."
> **Corollary 1**
> The trick is knowing what it depends on.
> **Corollary 2**
> If the answer to a question isn't "It depends,"
> then it's not a strategic question.

To illustrate what we mean, consider the question of whether a small business entering a new market should try to offer a high-quality or a low-quality product (relative to competitors). While one might reflexively answer "high quality is better," it's certainly not the case that companies selling higher-quality products are always more successful. To draw a familiar example from the Fortune 100: Walmart doesn't compete on quality, they compete on price, and they've identified a huge market of price-sensitive consumers who are very receptive to their offerings. Apple Inc.'s success story is the polar opposite—their products are never at the low end of the price spectrum, but Apple became the world's most valuable company by offering the highest available quality in the user experience. So, to a small business owner—should you act like a mini Walmart or a mini Apple? The answer, says Mazzeo's Law, is that it depends on the particulars of your company and its market.

In the chapters to come, we describe many interesting strategies that we heard about on the road, but we caution against simply copying the ones that worked. We think it's never enough to know *that* something worked; you need also to understand *why* it worked. Only then can you unpack the "it depends" and figure out if it will work for you. If that sounds complicated, well, we suppose it is. But none of the small business owners we talked to would describe their challenges as simple. The economic frameworks taught in leading MBA programs can help structure your thinking in the face of this complexity, and guide you to better decisions.

One final note about economics: If you took a high school or college economics class, and don't remember loving it… don't worry. We followed Mike's advice and took out all the math. (No graphs, either!)

The Division of Labor

What is it like to drive across America in a rental car with economists for the better part of a week? We hear you groaning, but it's really not that bad. After shifting roles a bit early on, we settled into a good routine by our third trip. Scott (the mop-headed George) drives while Paul (the kosher Sting) rides shotgun. The two bicker like an old married couple, with most fights breaking out over Paul's navigational skills. Somehow we manage to get lost quite a bit despite planning our routes carefully months in advance and having three GPS-equipped smartphones in the car. Paul blames Scott and Scott blames Paul, and Mike (Ben Stiller in a Yankees cap) secretly agrees with each when the other is out of earshot.

Mike rides in the back and has taken the role of audio

technician. As Scott drives to our next company visit, Mike transfers the sound file from our last interview to his laptop, which gives him a good excuse to tune out the argument in the front seat. (Scott: *Where the heck are we now, Magellan?*)

To Paul's frequent delight and Mike's constant chagrin, Scott as driver controls the radio, which we turn up on our evening city-to-city drives after rehashing the day's meetings. Boston, Kansas, and Sweet Home Alabama are more than just words on a highway sign to Scott. He and Paul are known, at times, to sing along with the likes of Journey and Foreigner, and argue about whether that last track was Boz Scaggs, Eddie Money, or Billy Squier. Mike, whose musical tastes are less refined, puts on headphones and tries to stream the Yankees game.

Planning a Roadside MBA trip is a group activity. We confer four or five months in advance to find a week when we're all free of various obligations. Then we negotiate over a good route, with each of us making proposals until a consensus winner emerges. Guided by Mike's desire to revisit some of the motels from his dissertation research and Scott's interest in off-the-beaten-path travel writers like William Least Heat-Moon, Neil Peart, and Dayton Duncan, we decided early on to stay (mostly) out of the big cities. So a good proposal involves two airports with four small cities or big towns in between.

Plan agreed upon, we gather at the first airport Sunday afternoon, motor that evening to our first town, meet with businesspeople all day Monday, then drive, usually around 150 miles, to the next town. Restaurant decisions rotate through the group, and dinner frequently consists of beer and something fried that our ex-wives would have discouraged us from eating back when we were married. For lodging, Mike and Paul often try to outdo each other by finding something with charm or character. Scott, however, actively dislikes both charm and character, preferring Holiday Inn Express. Scott has vetoed the entire bed-and-breakfast segment ever since an unsuspecting B&B owner in Ohio tried to engage him in conversation before he had finished his coffee. We hope she's OK.

But hey, enough of our yakkin'...Let's hit the road!

CHAPTER 1

Scaling a Business

Paul's concerns about whether we'd be able to find inter-esting small businesses vanished right at the start of our first trip. We met in Memphis, Tennessee, on a summer Sunday morning, and spent the day being tourists. We re-enacted the classic *Spinal Tap* scene at Elvis's grave, watched a hazy sunset with the ducks atop the Peabody Hotel, and popped Prilosec at 10:00 p.m. to counteract the horrifically bad BBQ platter we'd shared at a tourist trap on Beale Street.

We woke Monday to bright sunshine and grabbed a quick Holiday Inn Express breakfast. Hopping in our rented Dodge Charger, we headed northwest on US 63 to Jonesboro, Arkansas. Perched on Crowley's Ridge, a narrow band of hills rising above the flat and humid Mississippi River plain, Jonesboro boasts a population near 70,000. Arkansas State University, with plenty of newish academic buildings and dormitories, dominates the east side of town, and Stadium Boulevard was alive with dozens of newly constructed strip malls to serve a growing student population. Main Street, quieter with upscale restaurants in old brick buildings, sat a mile west of campus.

We were so excited to be out on the road that Paul and Scott were a little surprised when Mike suggested we stop for more coffee. "You didn't get enough brew at the hotel breakfast nook?" Scott asked, pointedly.

"Look, we have forty-five minutes until our next meeting. You'd rather just sit in the car?" Mike replied.

Paul navigated to the nearby Starbucks, where we resisted a strong urge to pepper the cashier and barista with business questions while ordering. Paul grabbed his tall coffee and waded through the late-morning crowd to a tiny round table near the front window. "Shouldn't we be at a hip independent coffee shop?" he asked after we had gathered. "I thought we were professors in search of small business stories."

"I'd say 'hip' is not a word that suits us," Mike quipped. "We're probably better off here."

"Cool people make me uncomfortable," Scott added, nodding.

The conversation quickly turned back to business (and away from our personal insecurities) as we contemplated how Starbucks has done it. It was, after all, a hip independent coffee shop at one time—one that grew to tens of thousands of outlets worldwide. This kind of success represents the promise and possibility of small business with aspirations for growth, and the Starbucks story began to frame our thinking about the companies we were planning to visit. Does this business have what it takes to expand, or are there factors present that will inherently limit its growth? What can companies do to grow effectively, and what pitfalls should they try to avoid? While it's not clear that we ever met with the next Starbucks, we did find many interesting companies that scaled up in creative ways. Others, however, struggled to grow despite having considerable success at a limited scale. An important Mazzeo's Law question for any small business owner is this: What does successful growth depend on?

Jonesboro, Arkansas
BRACES BY BURRIS DENTAL PRACTICE

Expand by Centralizing Common Activities to Lower Costs

Suitably caffeinated, we finished our crosstown Jonesboro jaunt and arrived at Braces by Burris, where we met with office manager Shawna Starnes. We were initially confused: The address indicated a white building in a small strip mall that appeared much larger than necessary for an orthodontist's office. When we went inside, we didn't see a lobby with nervous preteens waiting for their appointments as we had expected. Instead, there was a vast glassed-in area with cubicles surrounded by small offices.

"Welcome to the mother ship!" Shawna announced in greeting. Tall, slender, and wearing a stylish white pants suit, Shawna would fit right in as a recurring character on the hit TV show *Nashville*. We settled into her office for our interview, about to get a lesson in Arkansas geography.

"In addition to this, we have a practice in West Memphis that was purchased from an orthodontist there who was retiring," Shawna began in an energetic drawl. "We also opened a location in Forrest City. We have opened a practice in Blytheville. All these are about sixty miles from Jonesboro."

This list continued throughout the first fifteen minutes or so of our interview with Shawna. Over the past several years, Dr. Burris had increased the size of the practice by opening locations in new geographic areas and by opportunistically purchasing practices from doctors in other cities.

"Dr. Burris also bought a practice in 2007 from a doctor in Hot Springs, and that's our Central Arkansas practice. We have since opened three locations there as well."

By the time she was finished, Shawna had reeled off a total of eleven individual towns where the Burris team of ortho-dontists was present. It turned out that the Braces by Burris establishment we were visiting was the company's main loca-tion and the centralized hub that was coordinating activities throughout the region. Most of the towns that Burris has ex-panded into are relatively small, and the locations do not need to be open every day.

"We travel to the other locations on a rotating schedule," Shawna continued. "We're actually in the process of transi-tioning from two to three traveling teams—each team has two assistants along with someone to greet patients. We'll have dif-ferent orthodontists rotating into each of the different locations with different teams.

"Some of our days are long. Everything operates out of the Jonesboro location. We do have some equipment and tools on site, but for the most part we travel with our supplies. So, we load up in vans, and everyone leaves from here to go to our other sites. When we go to West Memphis or Blytheville or any of those locations, we'll start up at 7:15 and we might not get back 'til 6:15 or 6:30."

"And what happens here?" Mike asked.

"This location is our administrative office," Shawna replied. "Accounting, IT, HR. Billing, payments, and our call center are here. We have five people who answer the phones full-time. There are local numbers, but everything rings here. All the phones are answered the same way."

The Burris team grew by recognizing that while people don't want to travel too far to visit their orthodontist, the task of providing care requires little more than a small reception area and a couple of rooms where patients are seen. These stripped-down offices are very inexpensive to operate. The key to making a collection of satellite locations run smoothly is an efficient centralized hub that handles all of the support services for every location. Since billing and insurance are centralized, Braces by Burris saves a substantial amount by not employing someone at each individual office to manage these tasks. The practice has grown, in part, through serving state-funded Medicaid patients—Arkansas is one of the few states where Medicaid pays for orthodonture. Reimbursement requires state licensure and much navigating of bureaucratic red tape, which Burris's centralized system is well equipped to handle.

By utilizing its central office function across many satellite locations, Braces by Burris is employing the first principle of profitable growth: identifying and exploiting "economies of scale." Economies of scale exist if a company becomes more efficient as its unit volume (that is, its scale) increases. Three cost definitions are critical to understanding this concept. The first is average cost, which is simply the company's total cost divided by the number of units that it produces. Second is fixed cost, which are those costs a company incurs no matter how much it sells. Fixed costs typically include things like the rent on a building, the cost of equipment, and the price of a business license obtained from the state. The activities performed in the central office in Jonesboro largely represent fixed costs for Burris. Variable costs, our third definition, are those costs that a company must incur when it wants to produce additional output. At many businesses, inputs are important variable costs—an automobile manufacturer has to purchase four more tires for every car it sells. However, in some companies, variable costs can be quite low; Microsoft, for example, incurs very little additional cost when it sells another copy of the Office software package. Because it can utilize all the administrative functions in the central office, Burris's variable costs of operating its satellite locations are low.

It is precisely when fixed costs are high relative to variable costs that economies of scale are likely to be present. The logic is simple division: Total fixed costs remain constant as quantity increases, so the fixed cost per unit quantity falls. And when economies of scale are strong, growth leads to higher profits for two reasons: Quantity goes up *and* average costs go down. Imagine a scenario where you can increase your company's unit volume and earn a higher margin on each unit; any small business would jump on an opportunity like that.

Braces by Burris exploits economies of scale by centralizing back-office activities, and also in how it holds and tracks inventory—the metal brackets and wires that orthodontists implant in the mouth to straighten a patient's teeth. Shawna explained: "It is cost effective to keep the brackets and wires together in a single, central location. There's any number of different sizes of brackets—literally hundreds of inventory items. And we wouldn't want to stock every one of those hundreds of items in each location. It wouldn't be efficient to keep up with that inventory at every remote site where we go."

Over time, Braces by Burris has built up a system whereby it can effectively grow by expanding its practice into new locations without incurring too much in the way of additional costs. This allows the company to spread fixed costs over a larger and larger customer base and leads to powerful economies of scale.

Paul wondered aloud how far the Burris orthodontics empire might expand.

"One of our practices, in fact, is located about four hours from here," Shawna replied. "It is so small that we only go there once a month. We load up our plane and head down..."

It took Scott a minute to catch up. "Wait, did you say a plane? As in...airplane?"

"Yes. Dr. Burris himself flies. Once a month the team heads down to Central Arkansas on our plane. It's nice. It's very nice!!"

We certainly had not anticipated talking to an orthodontist's office with a corporate airplane!

Centralizing operations and sharing fixed costs are very important for Braces by Burris: By using the satellite office system, the Burris team can profitably operate in locations where a stand-alone orthodontist would fail. At the same time, the patients at these additional locations add up, ultimately producing greater overall efficiencies and growth for the business.

Denver, North Carolina
STEELE RUBBER PRODUCTS, INC.

Ensure That Revenue Opportunity Exceeds Fixed Costs

On a subsequent trip, we visited the community of Hickory, North Carolina, in the Piedmont region about an hour northwest of Charlotte. For many years, economic activity in Hickory centered on furniture manufacturing, taking advantage of the thick forests and ample transportation nearby. Though a good portion of that manufacturing has moved overseas, the city still draws over half a million visitors per year to its massive four-level Furniture Mart, with over one hundred showrooms and outlets. The local economy has diversified and now hosts a broad range of manufacturing and corporate employers, along with massive data centers from Apple, Google, and Facebook. After a lovely drive through winding forested hills from Hickory proper to the neighboring town of Denver (North Carolina), we met Matt Agosta, the president of Steele Rubber Products, Inc. We sat down at a small conference table in the office adjacent to the factory floor to talk to Matt, a sturdy man in his early sixties who wore a gray goatee and a maroon work shirt bearing the company logo.

Steele began in 1958 just outside Detroit, Michigan. Matt's father-in-law founded the company, which focused mainly on tool making to support the local automobile industry. He was also a vintage car collector and used the tools in his shop to make molds that could be used to fashion rubber parts and weather stripping. This is important to collectors because rubber parts become brittle as cars age. Over time, in partnership with a nearby rubber manufacturer, he produced these specialized rubber parts for friends in his vintage car clubs and eventually started offering them for sale to the public. With the oil crisis of the 1970s, demand for automotive tooling dried up, but the need for restoration parts grew. Steele decided to focus on the latter, making the move to North Carolina to take advantage of the warmer weather and a friendlier business climate. This is where Matt would eventually take over the business.

"When you look at a car," Matt explained, "it's amazing how many rubber pieces there are. You've got rubber parts that go around the glass to seal it, rubber that goes on a running board, rubber mounts for the engine to sit on ... Just about anywhere you have a light assembly sitting on a fender, there's a pad." As cars became more complex through history, the number of rubber parts increased substantially. Matt estimated that there were only about a dozen rubber parts on a classic Ford Model T, but, on a 1941 Cadillac, there might be three to four thousand dollars' worth of rubber pieces.

In describing the business—and the choices Matt needs to make to run the business effectively—one phrase came up over and over: "All the cost in the business is up front."

In other words, the company can't generate new streams of income without substantial initial investment.

This economic reality is the consequence of how Steele manufactures the replacement rubber parts. The process begins with a very important decision: Which particular model of classic car is Steele going to start manufacturing and selling rubber parts for?

"We are making parts for Pintos—that's probably one of the most unusual ones."

Mike had an extended flashback to his own childhood, being crammed along with his three sisters into his father's car. "We had a Pinto growing up. A red hatchback," Mike volunteered. "I can't really imagine anyone restoring and collecting one of those."

Paul laughed. "Didn't the Pinto have problems with fires and explosions?"

"Yes." Matt nodded. "And people ask, 'Why do you make parts for Pintos?' But they have a very strong club."

Once Steele has decided to provide parts for a particular car model, they've got to learn what rubber parts are inside the car. "We went and bought a Pinto," Matt described. "Found it at a local auction. Stripped the parts off of it and reverse engineered them. And then we made the parts to make sure that they'd fit. Tools have to be made for whatever we are trying to copy. Some parts are more than just rubber—they might have metal clips in the ends. They can get pretty complex."

The tooling process generates a metal mold for each of the 12,000 parts that Steele lists for sale in its catalog across hundreds of makes of car. The custom piece is the mold itself, which then fits into a machine where the rubber is vulcanized by applying heat and pressure to the dense raw material in the mold, forming the finished part. Touring Steele's facility, we saw a wide-open area where a few workers were quietly but diligently operating the machine tools and forming the new rubber parts. This work zone was lined by a series of tall shelves, which contained the company's extensive collection of molds that had been fashioned in the past and would be used to produce the actual rubber versions of the replacement parts to sell. Steele keeps a small inventory of the most popular parts on hand, but most parts are made to order. "We can't do it the mass-produced kind of way," Matt said, "since everything we do is in small numbers. But if I have the mold, I can make it pretty quick."

Making the mold represents the fixed cost of producing the part—the up-front investment on which the company will make its future earnings. And for Steele, these costs are substantial; the company must purchase the car, disassemble it, tool up the metal molds, manufacture rubber prototypes, and test fit. Once the molds are made, however, making rubber parts is relatively inexpensive. The additional cost is just the rubber, and these variable costs of producing additional output are small compared to the fixed costs. Strong economies of scale are present, so once Steele has made a mold, it benefits tremendously when more people buy these particular parts.

Since any set of molds can produce rubber parts for only a specific make and model of classic automobile, the decision to add a car to the product line represents a serious commitment. Unlike Braces by Burris, where fixed central-office costs don't need to be duplicated when satellite locations are opened, Steele incurs substantial new fixed costs when it adds a car to its catalog. Making this decision correctly requires a careful comparison of the costs of producing the molds and the potential market for sales of that car's parts in the future. To be successful, the company does a good deal of research to estimate what the size of the future restoration market might be before committing to produce a mold.

"We do research and see how many of those cars were

made. How well do they sell? And do they have anything else that makes them unusual or collectable or something that people like?" Matt explained. In the case of the Pinto, for example, Matt reported that Ford sold more than two million vehicles in the 1970s, and that demand from collectors remains strong, in spite of (or perhaps because of) the car's reputation as something of a lemon. If Steele's research indicates that the potential market is large enough, then a reasonable price can be set to cover the large fixed costs of making the molds and still generate a healthy profit.

The insight here is that to grow profitably, a company needs more than just economies of scale. Along with this feature—which really comes from the underlying manner in which the product or service is produced—it is critical that there is enough demand for that product or service. How much is enough? That depends on the level of the fixed costs. The benefits of economies of scale come from spreading those fixed costs over more sales, so the higher the fixed costs, the more sales you will need. If you build it (and pay the fixed costs of doing so) and they (the customers) don't come, the efficiencies never materialize.

Gresham, Oregon
SILK ESPRESSO CAFÉ

Expand Only Where Resources Can Be Shared

In our previous examples, we have seen the powerful effect that economies of scale can have on profits as businesses grow.

Mazzeo's Law, however, suggests that some companies will be better able to exploit economies of scale to expand their businesses than others. We saw two wonderful examples of the "it depends" of growth and scale when visiting a pair of seemingly similar food service operations—an Oregon coffee shop and a grill and bar headquartered in Mississippi. Their different experiences highlight the challenges associated with growth and can help guide your thinking on when expansion is a good idea.

While Mike was a coffee enthusiast during our day in Jonesboro, Arkansas, he had quit his six-cups-a-day habit—cold turkey—by the time of a subsequent trip to the Pacific Northwest. "I bought a juicer," Mike explained excitedly. "You guys should try celery juice with carrots, beets, and kale. It's amazing."

Paul and Scott stared open-mouthed as if Mike had said he was giving up his urbane Chicago apartment to live in a yurt. This was but one of several forays into "healthy eating" for Mike, who always seemed to be on some regimen or another. On one trip, he stuffed his briefcase with small Ziploc bags full of nuts and carrots that he ate instead of lunch. Another trip featured a detox plan called "The Clean." But coffee? This was as important a fuel as gasoline on Roadside MBA trips, and Paul and Scott soon determined that they didn't necessarily prefer the decaf version of Mike.

It was no help that we had scheduled a visit with an independent coffee shop. On a late afternoon in Gresham, Oregon, we pulled into a nondescript strip mall where we met with Silk Espresso owner and coffee aficionado Leah McMahon. A former varsity basketball player at Oregon State, Leah was now in her thirties but, with her straight brown hair and large silver leaf-shaped earrings, she would not have looked out of place on a college campus.

Though Leah told us that Gresham was part of the more rough-and-tumble "Eastside" of the Portland metro area, the atmosphere in the coffee shop belied that image. The décor was welcoming, and the Food Network was playing on the flat-screen television hanging on the wall. Both the clientele and the staff were very professional in their appearance and manner.

"We named the company based on what we wanted the end-user experience to be. We didn't just call it 'Cotton Espresso' or any other textile. It's silk. It's high level. It's upper echelon. We want the experience to be beyond what you were expecting."

True enough, Leah proudly reported that Silk Espresso had won a string of awards from the local press during the six years she had been in business. "I think we're up to seven awards now—Best Espresso, Best Café…" After having been, in her words, "spit out of the corporate world," Leah had certainly found her calling in the high-quality segment of the coffee market.

As we discussed the retail coffee business further, it became obvious that business survival requires dealing with the competition, specifically "the green giant up the road," as Leah put it.

"If we can come up with ways to be cool and relevant for a particular generation, the green giant isn't so powerful. We are thankful for them because their marketing affects us positively. We want to piggyback on that and say to customers, 'If you want award-winning, locally made, locally owned, locally operated coffee, we're right up the road.' We focus on questions like 'Are we worthy of Best Espresso?' and 'Are we worthy of Best Barista?' And we've been fortunate to be recognized."

While not quibbling with results, we were still puzzled. Mike pressed Leah for details: "What are the concrete steps you take to beat Starbucks on quality?"

"Are you coffee drinkers?" Leah asked impatiently, clearly a bit flummoxed by our ignorance and unaware of Mike's recent conversion. We were about to get a lesson in fine coffee from a pro's pro.

"OK, let me explain a little bit about coffee to you," she began.

Leah proceeded to describe a long list of factors that could affect the quality of an espresso drink. "Coffee has different things that can change it. Drastically. Some of the catalysts are temperature, humidity, and weather. The preparation of it—whether you're putting the espresso in the cup within fifteen seconds of its coming out of the machine. Are your beans coming from the right place? Are they stored properly? Are they ground properly? Is the temperature of your water correct? Are you double-filtering it?"

Silently, Paul and Scott wished that one-one-hundredth of this level of effort had been put into the motel coffee they had drunk earlier, while Mike wondered how temperature and humidity might be affecting his juicer.

"If all those hoops have been jumped through, then the finished product is good."

"OK, so how do you make it all happen?" Scott asked.

"The training is a big part of it," Leah replied. "It starts out with the fact that I am almost always here. There's always someone here who has the passion of an owner, who's hands-on. The end result is the highest quality."

"How much of your time is spent here at the store?" Paul asked.

Leah thought for a moment. "This is our lifestyle. I'm the opener, and my days go best if I get here at 4:45 a.m. On a good day I go home around 4:00 p.m., on a bad day, maybe sixish. I'm always on."

With so many steps necessary to produce the highest level of quality, it's important that Silk Espresso's owner is capable of incredible attention to detail. Indeed, Leah was among the most dedicated, hands-on owners that we visited on all of our road trips, and her extreme involvement is necessary, given the value proposition to consumers and how difficult it is to accomplish.

This is the kind of business model that, while very successful at a small scale, faces strict limits to growth. Silk Espresso had a large following of devotees and a great brand name in the community, so you might think these facts could support the opening of several outlets across Portland's Eastside suburbs. And in fact, Silk Espresso had grown to as many as four locations at one point.

But that put a huge burden on Leah since she needed to closely supervise operations at all four outlets to be successful. It was, of course, nearly impossible to do this effectively, and Leah was overwhelmed by trying to be everywhere at once. She likened a four-store chain of espresso cafés to an "empire." And so she scaled back. Silk Espresso is now back down to the single location in Gresham that we visited.

A key point here is that Leah's direct involvement is an essential resource for business success at Silk Espresso. Growth is inhibited because, unfortunately, Leah is not a resource that can be easily shared across multiple locations. In contrast, Braces by Burris did find ways to share key resources across locations, by leveraging centralized inventory control, billing, and expertise in Medicaid reimbursement across its various dispersed practices.

Hattiesburg, Mississippi
MUGSHOTS GRILL AND BAR

Seize Growth Opportunities You Can Monitor Remotely

Since Leah's struggle with adding Silk Espresso locations was connected to the challenges of scaling up high-quality monitoring, Mazzeo's Law suggests that successful scaling would be more likely in situations where quality isn't quite as important or where monitoring isn't as difficult. This contrast struck us immediately when we visited with Ron Savelle, the fast-talking, sharp-witted owner of a chain of Mugshots restaurants based in Hattiesburg, Mississippi. Ron tended bar at a local outlet of the national dining chain, Chili's, while a student at the nearby University of Southern Mississippi, and with his friendly manner and dimpled chin, it's easy to imagine him as the favorite barkeep of every sorority girl in town. We sat with Ron at an outdoor patio, and during our visit he frequently stopped midsentence to chat up a passing customer. He seemed as relaxed as Leah was intense.

After college—Ron said he graduated "a little late"—he and a friend went to Hawaii for six months "to goof off and chase women and have fun." "Out there," he continued, "we got the dream to open our own bar. The next January, we bought Mugshots. It was a night venue, crappy building, old and rundown, but it was ours and we loved it. We had made a name for ourselves on the night scene at Chili's, so people just followed us over, and we were a big hit right off the bat.

"My parents helped us buy the place, but we paid it off in four months," Ron said. "In August that year, I went up to Starkville, where Mississippi State is located, to see some friends. We went out to a bar, but it was closed and nobody could figure out why. So, five and a half weeks later we started out on our second Mugshots."

"Five and a half weeks?!?" Paul asked, as Mike and Scott chuckled.

"Yeah, I turned it around fast and within eight months of opening we had our second location," Ron added. "The Hattiesburg location was doing great, so we were just able to write a check to get it going in Starkville. We thought we'd go up there and do a night business like in Hattiesburg, but it turned into huge lunches and dinners. It was wild. The Starkville restaurant business took off, so we've opened every one of them since then as a restaurant. We opened Tuscaloosa the next year. We just finished our ninth year, and we have nine locations now."

Mike shook his head in disbelief at Ron's story. "Wait a minute...you open a restaurant, and it's a raging success. You open another one, and it's a raging success. This is not common."

"Being in college towns really helped us. When we got to Jackson," he said in rapid-fire speech, "you'd think it would have taken us forever to build our brand. But so many people in Jackson went to Mississippi State or Southern Miss or Alabama, or their kids went there, or they go there for football games on the weekends…Our name was branded very easily. I've probably got more money in my pocket right now than I've ever spent on advertising.

"If you're from Mississippi and you don't know Mugshots," Ron added, "well, you need to get out more."

While Mugshots' market is competitive with many national casual-dining chains such as Applebee's or Chili's, Ron has carved out a niche at a somewhat lower price point—which college kids probably appreciate. "Applebee's PPA (per person average) is probably $12 to $16, and we're more like $9 to $11. A place like that or Chili's, they have steaks and ribs. We try to keep it simple, use our hamburger patty and chicken breast as much as we can on sandwiches and salads. We get creative with ingredients, but with not a lot of stock in the back. We came up with the Peanut Butter Burger out on the tailgate of a truck while we were doing a catering job. We had a big jar of peanut butter and just put it on there, and it turned out to be awesome. Peanut Butter Burgers—you want smooth or crunchy?—they're in every restaurant we got. We sell a couple thousand a week.

"After a few years, my business partner and I decided to split up. I was married by then and starting to have babies, and we had some different ideas on how to do business," Ron said. "He took the locations in Starkville and Tuscaloosa, and he's been franchising other locations since. I took Hattiesburg and Jackson, and a year and half later I opened Biloxi and then Baton Rouge. I own all of my four locations."

"It's, what, 150 miles to Baton Rouge?" Paul noted, showing a mastery of geography not heretofore seen in our travels. "How do you keep tabs on things? Who makes decisions?"

"I hired Callie. She was my General Manager at Chili's when I worked there, and I hired her to work under me as an area manager. She goes around to all my stores and keeps an eye on them. She's in every store every week. Every day she's on the road, in a different store. She puts in six or seven good hours there.

"So what is Callie doing when she's on site?" Mike asked.

"We have a three-page checklist that Callie goes through. Picture frames, fans, floors, baseboards, cutting boards, knives, lettuce, down to everything, cooler space. The general manager has the list. Callie mixes up her schedule so they don't know when it's coming, but they know it's coming."

Ron supplements his checklist with other monitoring technologies that helped him scale Mugshots more efficiently. Operating at a lower price point, it's critical to keep costs down for Mugshots, and, as it turns out, one of the biggest costs of operating a bar is "beer shrinkage." Bartenders who take draws off the taps for pretty girls or their buddies (or themselves) can end up putting a large dent in your bottom line. Ron employs a technological solution that allows him to easily monitor this critical activity without being in any one of the restaurants.

"I get alerts on my phone if there's any suspicious activity. At all my stores we have between 18 and 33 beers on draft. There are microchips in each one of the taps and it tells me on my phone how many ounces of beer they just poured. It'll tell me if they poured 12 ounces and charged for a 10-ounce beer; it'll tell me if they poured a 22-ounce Foster's and charged for a Pabst. It tells me everything."

Sometimes employees make mistakes, so having this system helps the bartenders stay focused, according to Ron. They know that if they fill a pitcher but don't ring it up, they will be charged for it. In cases of outright theft, Ron has the information to discipline the offender.

"We had a guy from our monthly pest control. They do it overnight and at five in the morning an alert popped up on my phone. He poured himself a ten-ounce beer. It got him fired."

The monitoring technology and checklist epitomize why Ron is able to add locations to Mugshots more easily than Leah could for Silk Espresso. Recall that Ron has positioned Mugshots below main competitors like Chili's and Applebee's in terms of price point and quality, whereas Silk Espresso needed to maintain higher standards than Starbucks to attract customers. As a consequence, the items that need monitoring at remote locations are simpler and less nuanced—clean floors and crisp lettuce are enough to keep his customers happy. Because these items are straightforward, Ron can put them on a list and send a trusted employee with a clipboard on the road to make sure things are going reasonably well. Plus, if a restaurant runs out of chunky peanut butter and has to use smooth for a couple of days, the college kids looking for cheap burgers and beer probably won't be disappointed enough to take their business elsewhere.

Leah, on the other hand, devotes hours to training her

baristas and needs to keep a close watch on their activities. Pulling an espresso shot is a subtle skill that cannot be easily quantified, unlike the number of ounces of beer drawn from a tap. In economic terms, direct monitoring of activities by someone with a hands-on owner's mentality is an essential resource for success at Silk Espresso, and she cannot spread this resource across multiple locations as easily as Ron can.

This does not mean, however, that Leah cannot grow her business. Instead, it means she should seek growth opportunities that take advantage of the monitoring activity she is already doing at the flagship Silk Espresso location. Indeed, Leah did grow her business by supplementing coffee with pastries and sandwiches. Not surprisingly, given her attention to detail, she immediately began winning awards for these, too!

"I've been very committed to finding a quality product and making sure that it is something that I would serve my family and eat myself. It speaks to how meticulous we are about getting good things in here," Leah concluded. Her meticulous attention is difficult to extend outside one café, but she is able to manage multiple high-quality services so long as she can keep her eye on them directly.

As we pulled out of the parking lot at Mugshots, our conversation quickly turned to the comparison with Silk Espresso. After covering the deeper economic issues, we got to the menu. "I wonder if Leah's devotees would go for a peanut butter burger?" Paul joked.

"No way," Mike asserted. "It would have to be some kind of 'foodie' combination. Maybe a peanut butter, portobello, and goat cheese panini?"

"That sounds horrible," Scott said. "I'd prefer celery juice with beets and quail."

"Kale."

"Oh, sorry. What's that?"

Mazzeo's Law

Scaling a Business Profitably: What It Depends On

- **Economies of Scale:** The businesses in this chapter have been able to grow successfully by figuring out how to effectively spread out fixed costs when the business expands. On the surface, there are few notable similarities among these unique businesses, but they all have certain fixed costs that can be shared.

- **Adding Low Variable Cost Activities:** If the ratio of your fixed costs to variable costs in your business is high, you are in position to grow profitably. The clerical and inventory-related activities that Burris centralized in Jonesboro had sufficient capacity to accommodate even more practices without additional fixed expenditure and with minimal new variable costs.

- **Demand:** Even with a scalable model on the cost side, it is critical to have enough demand to offset the fixed costs needed to get the business up and running. Steele's costs of adding a car to its catalog are mainly up front, but they carefully research the market for potential collectors to ensure that they will sell enough rubber parts to cover the costs of making the molds.

- **Quality and Monitoring:** Silk Espresso's economies of scale don't extend to additional locations because high quality was necessary to compete successfully; and maintaining high quality required detailed, passionate supervision. Since Mugshots was competing at a lower price point, procedures and technology could effectively assist with monitoring, and Ron Savelle could profitably operate more locations in his growing chain.

CHAPTER 2

Establishing Barriers to Entry

It was Sunday night in Missoula, Montana, a beautiful city of 70,000 set in the spectacular Rocky Mountains, in an area known as "Big Sky Country". Mike and Paul had gathered at the Montana Club restaurant a block from our motel. As Paul checked the Rockies/Cardinals game on the big-screen TV above the bartender's head, Mike scanned the establishment, searching for their driver.

"Where's Scott?" Mike asked.

"He texted and said he got a late start. We should eat without him," Paul said.

Mike and Paul had flown in from their respective hometowns that afternoon, but Scott had decided to drive the 500-plus miles to Missoula from his base in Salt Lake City.

"Sounds fine," Mike said. "Why did he drive his car rather than fly and rent a car like usual?"

"He didn't say," Paul replied. "Hey, I'll buy you dinner if you get the Big Mike Burger—and finish it."

Mike eyed the menu and found the Big Mike: two one-third-pound all-beef patties, American cheese, and Thousand Island on a double brioche bun. "I'll take the Caesar salad with blackened salmon and a Big Sky IPA," Mike said when the waitress appeared, declining Paul's generous offer for fear of becoming, himself, a Big Mike.

Scott's late departure got him to Missoula well past midnight, and Mike and Paul were waiting impatiently outside his room the next morning.

"Is this Scott's car?" Mike said, pointing to a Volvo wagon with Utah plates in the Ruby Inn parking lot.

"Oh man," Paul sneered. "Is there anything less cool than three economists in a soccer-mom car?"

Just then, Scott emerged from his room. Over his shoulder, he carried a bicycle—a high-end, carbon-fiber, Lance-Armstrong-wannabe road bike. Speechless, Mike and Paul watched as Scott affixed the bike to the Volvo's roof rack. "Summer in Montana is perfect for biking. I'm figuring on some pre-meeting rides," he said, squinting in the early morning sun.

"OK, Rule #1," Paul lectured. "No Lycra bike shorts. I'm pretty sure I can speak for the entire Mountain Time Zone when I say I do not want to see you in those."

"Did your divorce decree say that she got the cool stuff and you got the Volvo?" Mike asked. "You should fire your lawyer."

Missoula is a college town, and we spent part of our day there at a start-up that was launched directly from the laboratory of a University of Montana chemistry professor named Donald Kiely. Professor Kiely had developed a process to produce a chemical compound called glucaric acid, and the start-up, Rivertop Renewables, was launched to try to find a market for the innovation. Unique among the companies we visited while on the road, this start-up owned technology that was protected from competition by a patent. A patent is a government-sanctioned monopoly that prevents rivals from copying the patent holder's methods—a powerful barrier to competitors wanting to enter the market. Patents exist to reward inventors; in exchange for disclosing the details of the innovation, the patent holder receives exclusive rights to use—and profit from—the innovation for a period of time.

Needless to say, this is a pretty good deal if you can get it, but few small businesses are built around patentable innovations. And this means that competition—share-stealing and margin-destroying competition—is a fact of life for most small businesses. Our MBA students frequently pitch their business ideas to us during office hours, and a stock question we ask in response is "What would prevent competitors from copying your idea, entering your market, and stealing a big chunk of your profits?" Without barriers to entry, even the best business strategies will only temporarily generate great results.

Different markets do, however, present different challenges to entrants, and it's useful to anticipate which markets are likely to quickly become crowded with competitors—and hence unprofitable—and which are not. An important Mazzeo's Law question for all businesspeople is this: Can I erect barriers to entry to protect my business from margin-destroying competition?

Jonesboro, Arkansas
WILCOXSON'S KIDS PLACE

Be First When the Market Isn't Big Enough for Two

During our day in Jonesboro, we met with Doug Wilcoxson, owner of Wilcoxson's Kids Place. In his mid-thirties and clad in a black polo with his store's logo—the polo shirt people are making a mint off small business owners, judging from what we saw on the road—Doug Wilcoxson smiled shyly and began speaking with a soft Southern drawl. "I grew up in the furniture industry. My grandpa started a store in 1946, and he, my dad, and my uncle all worked at the store up in Kennett, Missouri, about an hour from here. After I got married and had twins, I thought I'd open my own store."

Doug's business is small even for a small business; his sole employee, Terry, puttered in the storeroom while we talked. But it is the biggest kids' furniture store within sixty miles. That's because it is the *only* kids' furniture store within sixty miles. After college and a few years in the family business, he began exploring opportunities to open his own store. During this search, as Doug tells it, "My wife said, 'What about a children's furniture store?' I did a lot of research. I went to Memphis, Little Rock, Saint Louis, Springfield—those were the closest places to find specialty stores, a furniture store for kids. When we had our twins, there was nothing here. It is tough to find baby furniture if you don't have a specialty store." Part of Doug's market research was talking with his friends who were having babies. "The guys would all say, 'Aww man, we gotta go to Memphis this weekend to go look for *baby furniture.*'" (Spoken with contempt as if the guys had nothing to do with the fact that a baby was imminent.)

Doug opened in 2006 in downtown Jonesboro, focusing on cribs, strollers, and car seats, but has since moved to a newish brick-facade strip mall just a few blocks from the Arkansas State football stadium. His product knowledge, we learned, is extensive, coming both from his experience in his grandfather's store and also from using many of the products with his own three children. And he makes significant investments in maintaining that knowledge. "ABC Expo in Las Vegas," he said, "is the biggest kids' expo; all the vendors of kids' stuff meet there once a year to exhibit. I get help in the store, and I go for two days. I walk probably thirty miles each day to talk to the right vendors. Probably 65 percent of my sales are special order; a customer comes in, sees something in the shop but it's not exactly what they need. If I can get that customer talking, I can usually visualize what they need and then special order something I saw at market."

Doug combines this depth of knowledge with personal service. He does all deliveries himself using the custom-painted trailer he keeps parked out front as a pseudo-billboard, and while he says he doesn't always remember customers' names, he can always remember what crib they bought.

Doug has a powerful barrier to entry because, though there is significant demand for specialty kids' furniture in the Jonesboro area, there is not so much demand that a second store might open. When Doug opened, his research suggested that there was enough demand for specialty kids' furniture in the area that he could make a decent living as long as he had the market to himself. But could Doug reasonably assume that he would have the market to himself? Did he have an answer to the question we ask our students about entry putting pressure on prices?

To answer that question, let's adopt the point of view of a potential entrant that might open a business that is "close" to Doug's store both in terms of physical proximity and the products and services the entrant might offer. The new rival could expect, at best, to split the Jonesboro market with Doug's already-established shop. Given the small size of the market overall, a rival would be unlikely to make a decent living as one of two kids' furniture stores in Jonesboro. Anticipating that entry would be unsuccessful, the potential entrant will likely choose another line of business—one that does not compete with Doug's.

In essence, Jonesboro ain't big enough for the both of them. Thinking into the future this way, Doug knew that he would be the only store like his when he opened and that he could expect it to remain that way for some time.

A market like kids' specialty furniture stores in Jonesboro—where one producer can be profitable but two cannot—is a "natural monopoly." A canonical big business example of a natural monopoly is cable television. The situation there is different, though, because the reason cable television is a natural monopoly has more to do with costs than with market size. For cable TV, entering a market comes from the need to install a massive network of underground cable. Even for very large cities, the split-the-market profit is likely to be too small to induce a second business to make such a large entry investment. In response, cities and towns typically grant monopoly rights to a single cable provider but then directly regulate prices to stop the monopolist from gouging customers.

Whatever the basis for a natural monopoly, the essential strategy point is the same—you want to get there first. A pre-existing rival for Doug would have been enough to deter his entry. Doug was the first to open, though and, as long as he is around, additional entry is unlikely.

Of course, that doesn't mean Doug is on easy street. Doug's advantage applies only to customers who insist on buying kids' furniture at a specialty store; for the rest of the market, he must compete. "Our main competition now is Walmart, Target, and online," he said. "I love it when people tell me about their trip to Babies R Us in Memphis. They'll say 'They had so many products, and the staff didn't know anything about them.' That's why I'm in business." Doug has a strong barrier to entry in the local specialty kids' market, but he still invests heavily in product knowledge and service to compete with the big-box stores and Amazon.

Dothan, Alabama
KEY FIRE HOSE

Go All-In with Irreversible Investments

Charlie Genthner, owner of Key Fire Hose in Dothan, Alabama, kept us laughing as he shared another great barriers-to-entry story with us. A large man whose gruff voice seemed out of place given his ever-present smile, Charlie sported a well-worn red polo displaying the Key Fire Hose insignia. His assistant, Marla, brought coffee as we sat down to chat in his brightly decorated office.

"I started with BFGoodrich out of college," he began. "I was an engineer and chose their fire hose division because it's a good product, everybody needs it, and there's hardly any competition. Even then I wanted to go into business for myself and thought this would be a good business to learn."

After a lateral move to a competitor and a 1987 corporate buyout, Charlie was asked by his employer's new owner to sign an agreement not to start a competing business. He declined and found himself unemployed just weeks before Christmas. Determined not to be a buyout victim again, Charlie went back into the fire hose business, this time in partnership with two old colleagues. "We wrote a nice business plan," he said. "Well, it would probably have gotten a B+ from you guys."

We laughed as Mike tried to slow Charlie down. "Waaait a minute! We'll be the judge of that."

Over time, Charlie gained full control over Key Fire Hose, and he now employs nearly 150 people. "I have a mentor who used to tell me 'Charlie, there are three things you want: A piece of the action, a bigger piece of the action, and then all of the action.'"

Laughing again, Scott asked "So how do you make fire hose?"

"And what makes one fire hose better than another?" said Paul.

"There's a fabric jacket made by a loom, and inside the jacket is a rubber tube that we extrude," Charlie explained. (An extrusion process pushes liquefied rubber through a mold to create the tube.) "The customer is always wanting a light product for when the fireman is carrying it up stairs. Obviously it can't kink, but it has to fold when it's not in use. The jacket has to be strong and abrasion resistant. I'm always managing trade-offs."

Mike raised a pricing concern: "I'd be worried that the people buying fire hose are government bean counters looking to save money."

"If one man dies in New York City on the fire line," Charlie replied, "it costs that city over two million dollars. One guy gets hurt, it's over a million dollars. Their injuries since they started dealing with me have been almost zero. They've done the mathematics of this. Our political leaders aren't *all* totally dense."

Donning ear and eye protection, we saw the looms in operation on a quick plant tour with Charlie's son, Burke. A massive cylindrical machine, a fire hose loom pulls polyester thread from spools located around the edges. A moving circular assembly in the center of the machine forms the thread into a tubular fabric jacket. Charlie's plant had twenty looms running—together producing more noise than The Who circa 1969—with only a few workers around making sure things were running smoothly.

"The heart of this business is the looms. When I started, the looms were about $75,000 each and you needed about ten of them. So you needed $750,000 of capital equipment and another half a million for working capital to get the flow going. There's very little labor in a fire hose. Your capital equipment is what constricts your growth. Today a loom is $150,000. The only thing you can do with a fire hose loom is make fire hose. Otherwise, it's a boat anchor."

Charlie's comparison of a fire hose loom to a boat anchor may have been the most apt metaphor we heard on all our journeys. The reason is that a fire hose loom is a sunk cost. "Sunk" doesn't mean "submerged" (as in boat anchor), but rather "irreversible." A sunk cost is a cost that, once incurred, cannot be undone. When Charlie orders a loom, he's turning cash, a valuable resource that can be flexibly deployed into any number of markets, into a fire hose loom. A fire hose loom is valuable too, but this loom cannot be redeployed outside of the fire hose market.

Sunk costs generate strong barriers to entry. To see why, think about how Charlie, with his sunk investment in looms, would likely respond to the entry of a new player in the hose market. Entry would mean more competition and lower prices in the fire hose market. Charlie's business could easily become unprofitable when factoring in his high capital costs, but what are his options at that point?

He can't get his money back from the loom maker. He could liquidate and try to sell his looms, but who's going to buy, given the lower prices in the fire hose market? It is very likely that Charlie would respond to entry by doing nothing; that is, by continuing to produce the exact same amount of fire hose he would have produced without the entry. Even if he's losing money when factoring in his massive investment in looms, that investment is sunk. It's spent. It's water under the bridge. (OK, enough water metaphors...)

A company that has incurred sunk costs is fully committed to the market. It's all in, with no going back, no turning around, no alternative to sticking it out. And this level of commitment can be quite discouraging to entrants. An entrant looking at fire hose knows that, no matter how bad things might get for Charlie, he's always better off making fire hose with his looms than shutting them down. Sunk costs mean Charlie will be a tenacious competitor for any entrant, and this makes entry less attractive than it would be otherwise. Things would be quite different if looms could be redeployed outside the industry. Facing an aggressive and efficient new competitor, Charlie might well be tempted to sell looms to a buyer outside the fire hose industry if the machinery could be redeployed to make other textiles.

Investments in physical capital are but one potential source of sunk costs; Charlie's own *human capital*—that is, investments he's made to acquire knowledge and build relationships—is another. Mike asked just the question to illustrate: "How did you acquire customers when you first went out on your own?"

"Oh, I know everybody," Charlie replied. "An old customer called me up after I left my last company and said, 'What are you going to do?' I was forty-two years old and I had two kids in college so. I said, 'I don't know what else to do. I gotta make fire hose.'" Charlie's unwillingness to consider careers outside the fire hose industry is another illustration of the sunk cost principle. His investment of twenty years in learning how to engineer, make, and sell fire hose was sunk. The industry is sufficiently specialized that there was no earning a return on that investment elsewhere, so he had little choice but to stay in and fight.

The key to building a barrier to entry in markets like this is to make sunk cost investments before competitors do. Sinking the costs turns you into a ferocious competitor, and it's this transformation that deters entry.

This race to invest first was being played out in a new market around the time we visited with Charlie. The use of hydraulic fracturing (fracking) to extract oil and gas was growing rapidly throughout the United States. Fracking requires a very large and extremely reliable hose, basically a larger-diameter version of what Key Fire Hose makes for fire departments. You might think that this represents a great business opportunity for Key, and Charlie thinks it does—in the short term. As this market grows, however, it will attract investment, and that investment in additional looms is again a sunk cost that will deter future investments. A race to invest in loom capacity is likely to ensue.

"That market is staggering," Charlie told us. "I'm just a little tiny pimple, but I'm very important because the whole thing doesn't work without my hose. Now, is it going to last? Nah. Markets that favor the seller don't last very long in a free enterprise system." Charlie's strong position in fire hose gives him a head start in the fracking hose business. But developing those same long-term advantages and barriers to competition in the fracking business are a challenge that could put Charlie and Key Fire Hose to the test.

Marietta, Georgia
PRODEW INC.

Leverage Scale to Hit an Unmatchable Price Point

A long drive left us at a Holiday Inn Express just off US 41 in suburban Atlanta, in a fairly crowded area with many large retail stores and office buildings. We were tired but also hungry, exactly the conditions that favor a catastrophic restaurant mistake. After dropping our bags, we met in the lobby, each of us scouring our phones for dining options.

"We're just across the Perimeter from Cumberland Mall. Food court, anyone?" Mike asked, sarcastically.

"Downtown Atlanta has lots of options, but that'd mean another half hour in the car," Scott said.

"I'm making an executive decision," Paul declared. "There's a chain Italian just two blocks that way. How can you screw up pasta?"

Famous last words. In our travels, we have seen firsthand the many ways to botch, bungle, and bollix simple Italian food: grease (as we saw in Missouri), overcooking (Iowa), and even bizarre décor (Oregon). The culprit in Georgia was oversalting, which was so bad that Paul was up half the night just trying to stay hydrated. No doubt Mike's ancestors spent this particular evening spinning in their graves.

Groggy the next morning, we nevertheless made it to Prodew Inc., which is housed in a nondescript warehouse in Marietta. Things quickly turned for the better when we met the company's founders, Itamar Kleinberger and Shakeel Merchant. Not only did they offer us donuts in addition to coffee—Scott took two—they had also written out several pages of notes in preparation for our interview. Itamar, fiftyish with an Israeli accent, led us to a conference room, while Shakeel, tall and late thirties, followed behind.

"We manufacture the misting systems in supermarkets," Itamar began. "The spray on the vegetables and the 'thunder' that warns shoppers the spray is about to begin? I was involved with a previous company that made systems, and when my non-compete ended in 2001, Shakeel and I decided to join forces and start a company in the same area."

At the time, Itamar explained, four companies split the US market for misting systems, and dominated internationally as well. "We're now in all the major chains," he said proudly, "and some of them, like Kroger, use only us. Walmart, we probably have 70 percent of their stores."

"How did you enter against established players?" Scott asked between bites.

"We asked ourselves 'What are our advantages?'" Itamar said. "First, we're both engineers. The competition doesn't have engineers. They're using old technology. Second, supermarkets work on net profit of around 3 to 4 percent."

Shakeel added, "If you buy fifty-nine dollars in groceries, the supermarket makes about a dollar."

Itamar nodded. "If you come with a product that is as good as or better than what's in the industry with considerably lower cost, then you can get in."

"Third, Itamar was the main engineer at one of the four established players before he left," Shakeel said. "People in the industry knew him, and that really helped open doors. We weren't just guys coming in off the street."

Impressed, Mike asked "How did you get to the lower cost? Are your systems different?"

The pair explained that the competing products use an extruded rubber tube as the main mist track. An installer must cut tube to fit as part of the installation process, then holes must be drilled to screw in various nozzle heads. "We came up with a totally different concept. We decided to mold everything and do heat injection. Here's a twelve-inch piece, nine-inch," Itamar said, picking up samples from the conference table. "It's like a Lego, it all clicks together."

"Much cheaper to ship because of the weight," Shakeel added. "Easier to maintain. Will not break often. It's easier to install. We call it 'plug and spray.'"

"See here?" Itamar asked, holding up a sample of a competitor's product (he was exceedingly well prepared for our interview—with props even!). "Small hole for water to enter with extrusion. We have a big hole with molding. We run a hundred-foot system on one connection and still get even pressure distribution. The old system would need multiple connections, so it's much harder to install."

"And what was your pricing strategy to enter?" Paul asked.

"We needed to capture a very big share of the market," Itamar replied. "That was our first thought. It's only when we have quantity that we can afford the molds and the manufacturing and the production and everything. If a misting system used to be somewhere between two and three thousand dollars, we brought it down to below a thousand."

Smiling, Shakeel said "And *that* got everyone's attention."

Mike nodded, thinking back to the scale economics of injection molding at Steele Rubber in North Carolina. Like Steele, Prodew builds a custom mold for every part it hopes to sell, and this means that much of the cost of the business is up front. Unlike Steele, Prodew outsources the actual injection molding work. As Shakeel said, "We're not a plastics company."

Our discussion then turned to the response by the four existing competitors. "Do you have patents to protect this technology?" Mike wondered.

Itamar shook his head. "Patents cost a lot of money, very expensive to protect your ideas."

"Don't you worry that your competitors will hook up with manufacturing in Asia?" Paul asked.

Picking up a piece of Prodew plastic, Scott added, "You've handed them the blueprint right here."

Unconcerned, Itamar replied. "Here's the thing. To do any product in injection, you need to have the quantity. If they don't have big quantity, it doesn't justify it for them to make it. Shakeel and I, pretty much from the beginning, have been focused on acquiring a very big share of the market."

Prodew's strategy to prevent rivals from copying them is simple but ingenious. They realize that there is no legal or technological barrier to entry; they've not filed for a patent, and they're using off-the-shelf plastics technology. Rather, they've recognized that their injection molding approach is cost effective only at a very large scale. Recall that when economies of scale are present, average costs fall as quantity increases. A company at or above the minimum efficient scale (the quantity at which average costs are minimized) will always have a cost advantage over one that is below the minimum efficient scale; the smaller business will simply not have the scale necessary to get costs low enough to compete.

Prodew's strategy leverages exactly this insight. To erect a barrier to entry, they must find ways to keep rivals below the minimum efficient scale. And the best way to keep rivals underscaled? Simply grab up all the market share for yourself! Prodew could likely have made more money—in the short run—by pricing less aggressively and earning higher margins. This, however, would have left room in the market for a competitor to expand and possibly gain enough scale to become a credible competitor with a copycat injection-molded product. Instead, Prodew undercut rivals substantially on price to grab share and maintain their long-run advantage.

As Itamar put it, "We didn't want to be rich from one sale. We looked long term: Where are we going to be in five years? We did our pricing accordingly, with a target to have quantity."

By moving first with a lower-cost innovation, Prodew grabbed a lot of share and drove its costs down. Its competitors and other potential entrants could not justify going through the costs of developing a new, similar product without some assurance that they could grab a lot of that share back from Prodew. As a result, Prodew had erected a strong barrier to entry.

Pensacola, Florida
COLLEGEFROG

Don't Use Facebook, BE Facebook

Marooned far at the western edge of the Florida panhandle, Pensacola has experienced rapid growth in recent years. The metropolitan area now boasts almost half a million people, buoyed by a large naval base and a thriving tourist industry (at least between major oil spills). To reach our hotel, we drove past miles of strip-mall sprawl, much of which was built during a real estate boom of the 1990s and early 2000s. Hoping a larger city might have more extensive ethnic food options, we dodged the chains to try our luck with Vietnamese. After some quick smartphone research, we ended up in what must be the Southeast Asian part of town on North Davis Highway.

"I see Pho Golden Palace. Oh, and there's Tu-Do Vietnamese. Which one?" Mike said.

"An Asian meal in the deep South has been on my to-do list for a while," Paul joked. "I say we do Tu-Do."

This time, Paul's flip decision was a huge success, as Tu-Do served us a delicious, spicy dinner involving squid, mint, *bun* (which the menu helpfully describes as Vietnamese vermicelli), and a few bottles of imported beer. While dinner worked out well, exercise the next morning was a bit of a disaster. Mike had forgotten to pack athletic socks for his usual morning workout and turned up at the Hampton Inn gym in shorts and dress socks. Paul tried to talk him out of it: "Mike, you can't do it. People come to us for business advice. Who's going to take the advice of a guy who exercises in dress socks?"

"If you have concerns about wardrobe and credibility, I'd suggest you start with Mr. Lycra Bike Shorts," he said, putting on headphones to tune Paul out.

After breakfast, we drove to a local office park that caters to fledgling businesses. Once there, we met with the leadership team of CollegeFrog, a tech start-up that is trying to transform college recruitment and hiring in the stodgy world of accounting. Jeff Phillips, James Hosman, and Frank White are partners and hold leadership roles at the company. Bright, clean-cut, and in their early thirties, the trio looked a lot like the ambitious young MBA students we work with on a regular basis.

We found this visit to be particularly enjoyable because it allowed us to make accountant jokes. Accountants are the only group who make economists seem exciting, so we have to take our shots when we can.

Jeff began the meeting by outlining the CollegeFrog business model. "It's a web-based application. Half of it is a jobs noticeboard; think Monster.com for college students and entry-level jobs. The other half is an applicant-tracking system that automates many of the steps of recruitment and eliminates waste."

"Ninety percent of the people hired each year in the accounting industry are straight from college," Frank continued, "and our goal is to streamline the recruiting process. Everybody knows the Big Four accounting firms; they are the absolute masters of college recruiting. But there are five or six thousand accounting firms in the country, and we want to take what the Big Four do and bring it to the next five thousand."

"We collect résumés from students and build a totally searchable database," James added. "Suppose a firm wants somebody who has Beta Alpha Psi experience, which is the accounting fraternity. They can search for that once they're a subscriber."

"Wait..." Paul said. "There's an accounting fraternity?"

"Imagine the parties," Mike quipped.

"It's an honor society," Scott corrected. "Think Phi Beta Kappa. I've been to a meeting of the Utah chapter."

"I bet the Utah chapter has even better parties. Did you wear a toga?" Paul asked.

"So many accounting jokes," Jeff said through a strained smile, obviously having heard all of them seven or eight thousand times.

If a college senior wants to get a job as an accountant,

she (most new accountants are women) sends her résumé to the firms she knows. Colleges help with placement as well, often publishing a book of students' résumés and sending it out to local firms. On their end, accounting firms looking for employees typically visit a few local schools and do a day of on-campus recruiting. This process leaves much to be desired, however, since both sides may miss out on good matches by searching too narrowly. Using online search, CollegeFrog is trying to make it easier for both sides to find each other, especially if they are not in the same geographic area. To do this, however, they need to do two things: They need to attract accounting firms to post jobs, and they need to induce aspiring accountants to post their résumés.

Jeff described the Facebook-like plans at CollegeFrog. "We are trying to become *the network* for accounting talent in college. We are becoming the expert on the recruiting process in this industry. The idea is, once that network effect kicks in — once we have enough students and enough firms — then it will be the place everybody comes because that's where everybody else is. We think there's value in that network itself."

During our time on the road, many business owners told us they are "on Facebook" trying to develop a brand presence through social media. But CollegeFrog is one of a smaller set of companies that is using Facebook as a model for developing entry barriers. Facebook protects its market position by utilizing what economists call a "network effect." Consumers are attracted to Facebook partly by the service itself, but even more by the size of the network of other users. What good would it do any of us to post banal commentary and silly pictures on a timeline that none of our friends can see? It's a wonderfully virtuous cycle: The more people that go to Facebook, the more people want to go to Facebook.

For Facebook, network effects generate the ultimate entry barrier. Once Facebook became established as the leading social networking site, it became difficult for others to acquire users and enter the market. After all, who would choose to join a brand-new site with no friends to find? Entrants face a network-effects conundrum: In order to attract users, you must first have users, so it's practically impossible to get going.

Network effects are not exclusively the province of Internet businesses. Consider, for example, shopping malls. Stores want to open in malls that have a lot of shoppers, and shoppers want to go to malls that have good stores. If there is a well-established mall in an area, it is difficult for a new mall to make inroads. Why should a store open there instead of taking advantage of the critical mass of shoppers at the existing mall? The network effects at work here are somewhat more subtle than in the Facebook example. Shoppers go to where the other shoppers are not because they value the presence of other shoppers directly, but instead because a critical mass of shoppers helps to attract stores. It is precisely this indirect effect that CollegeFrog hopes to exploit: A critical mass of accounting students will attract firms, and vice versa.

Should CollegeFrog limit itself to the accounting market and to new college graduates? If the network effects work for accounting, they should, in principle, also be relevant for teachers, engineers—really the whole hiring market. But just as Facebook spread its network slowly from one college to another and, after some time, to the broader public, CollegeFrog is trying to create strong networks one market at a time.

Jeff explains, "We got some very good input from one of our advisors early on who said, 'You guys really need to develop your product in one industry, focus on that industry well, own it, and then expand into other industries.'"

When we met with CollegeFrog, they were at a crucial point in their growth. They had just sent out bills to their initial subscribers and were waiting to see if anybody would pay them. Had they hit the critical mass of students where the firms felt they had to be part of it? If so, they could start reaping the benefits of the network they had developed and watch it grow. Better yet, they could start thinking about other markets besides accounting. But we had bad news for the guys at CollegeFrog—there's already a well-established system for hiring PhD economists.

We thanked Jeff, James, and Frank and walked out into bright late-morning sunshine, accompanied by a cool sea breeze. We quickly agreed that the CollegeFrog business model has a compelling barriers-to-entry logic, assuming that the company can secure sufficient numbers on both sides of the market. This led us into a discussion of whether our own plan—to become world-class traveling strategy gurus for the small business community—could similarly become immune to competition. Then it hit us—no, not the great idea to keep rival roving trios of business professors from copying us. Rather, it was the scent of Mike's double-duty socks coming from the back seat. Our willingness to drive all over, stay at mediocre hotels, and—most importantly—put up with each other for days at a time is unique in the world of academic economists. Yes, for authors at least, low standards can be a great barrier to entry.

Mazzeo's Law

Establishing Barriers to Entry: What It Depends On

- **Market Size and Entry Costs:** Wilcoxson's Kids Place is likely to be the only kids' furniture store within an hour's drive for a long time. The owner of a second store in this market would be unlikely to earn a decent living so Doug's presence is a barrier to entry.

- **Sunk Costs:** Key Fire Hose requires large investments in specialized looms that can only make fire hose. No matter how bad things might get, Charlie Genthner is always better off making fire hose with his looms than shutting them down, and this means that it will be next to impossible for an entrant to drive Charlie from the market.

- **Minimum Efficient Scale:** A company at or above the minimum efficient scale will always have a cost advantage over one that is below the minimum efficient scale. After developing a new injection-molded misting system, Prodew priced aggressively to grab share and keep potential copycat entrants from attaining the minimum efficient scale.

- **Network Effects:** If CollegeFrog can become the go-to site for aspiring accountants and the firms that seek to hire them, it will have built up a huge barrier to entry. Network effects, where demand creates demand, are very hard to overcome.

CHAPTER 3

Product Differentiation

"**A**re you sure you want to do this?"

"Yes."

"We can cancel and head home."

"If I go home, I'll just sit there and feel bad at home. Might as well feel bad here and ruin your day too."

So began our day in Frankfort, Kentucky. We had learned at dinner the previous night that Paul's beautiful golden retriever, Opus, had died unexpectedly after an emergency surgery. With their own beloved dogs (Bert for Mike, Rusty and Mēna for Scott) back home, Mike and Scott felt Paul's pain acutely. After a solemn dinner, we decided to confer in the morning on whether to continue with our trip or cancel and try again when our spirits were higher. After breakfast Paul seemed up for continuing, although it didn't look like he had slept much. We soldiered on, but the spring sunshine and blossoming trees did little to brighten our moods.

Our first meeting didn't help matters. Mike, having somehow given the local Chamber of Commerce the wrong impression of our project, led us to a dark coffee shop across from the Old State Capitol. There we met with a diverse group of downtown shopkeepers who, it seemed, had been coached to talk about nothing other than how wonderful Frankfort is— well, except for the near total lack of foot traffic when the legislature isn't in session. In any event, we didn't learn much about the strategic challenges facing these businesses, and it was a wasted ninety minutes.

This was rapidly becoming the Worst Day in the History of Roadside MBA.

But, as any experienced traveler knows, it's precisely when things are going sideways that you're likely to get an unexpected lift. Enter Diana Geddes, owner of Fit Time for Women, and the savior of our day in Frankfort. Friendly, funny, and somewhat puzzled by the three economists at her door, Diana is a state-government retiree who bought Fit Time as a second career after exercising there herself for years.

Diana got us laughing—no easy feat on this day—but, more importantly, got us thinking hard about product differentiation. Most small businesses cannot compete on price alone—only a company with the lowest costs in its market could do so profitably. But a business that has successfully executed a product-differentiation strategy can potentially charge a higher price than its competition without losing customers. Why would customers stay even if prices are higher? The key is to offer something different from what others offer. If your customers have a strong attachment to what you offer and find it superior to what your competitors offer, they may willingly pay more, enhancing your profitability.

Figuring out how to differentiate successfully is a challenge for most businesses—as Mazzeo's Law implies, the right approach will depend on the competitive situation that you face. In this chapter, we tell the stories of several businesses like Diana's that used creative ways to address the specific challenges of their market and compete effectively using a product-differentiation strategy.

Frankfort, Kentucky
FIT TIME FOR WOMEN

Find Your Target Customers, Identify Their Critical Needs

Brighton Park Shopping Center sits east of downtown Frankfort, with Kroger's supermarket serving as the anchor tenant. Besides Kroger's, the largest storefront belongs to Fit Time for Women, where we met Diana, an athletic woman in her early sixties with straight auburn hair and a wide smile. We certainly got a few strange looks when we entered and inquired at the reception desk—a group of three men don't enter this establishment all that often. When we sat down to talk with Diana, we learned about how specifically catering to female gym-goers defined her business and generated opportunities for product differentiation.

The niche itself is simple enough to describe. "The gym is women-only," Diana put it plainly. Frankfort has two other gyms—the Y and another independent facility—both of which are co-ed. Her customers value the ability to exercise without men present.

"A lot of these ladies, a lot of my clients, are older. And they don't want 'em," Diana went on, referring to men. She was so friendly and charming that we did not take offense.

"These ladies feel pretty comfortable back here. I've got one class at noon that's held in a chair. My mother takes it, and she's eighty-four." We wondered if Diana charges her mother but figured it was impolite to ask.

"I've got them coming in on walkers. I mean, most gyms don't want these folks," Diana said with a hearty laugh. "They just don't want them."

"I have a couple of 'ladies of faith' that come into the gym with covered heads and unwrap to exercise. We have to be very careful—that's why these doors are wooden," Diana explained, pointing behind her. Unlike many gyms that have a glassed-in workout area, the view was blocked from where we were seated in the front of the building. "You can't see back there, so they feel comfortable."

"Men can do anything up front; the gym is women only," Diana clarified.

The wooden door is just one of the ways Diana has tailored the services offered at Fit Time to cater to her female customers. Child care, for example is a must, "You have to have it if you're all girls! I have a shift from nine to twelve every morning Monday through Saturday, and four to eight Monday through Thursday."

It is a relatively expensive service to provide but one that is absolutely necessary. "I have to have two staff members available at all times so someone can be in here if there are kids."

"I thought the TV was enough," countered Scott, reflecting the values of those of us not welcome at Fit Time.

"Sometimes there are no kids in there, and I have to pay someone anyway, so it's a big expense," Diana went on, ignoring the male suggestions. "Retired ladies—grannies in training—in the morning; high school girls in the afternoon."

Fitness classes are also crucial. "We teach about thirty-six to forty per week," Diana explained, "That's my big pull. It's in their membership, but I do sell a lot of day passes to ladies— from other gyms even—to take my classes."

Cleanliness of the facility is also extremely important to the customers of Fit Time, and Diana and her staff pay close attention to making sure that the gym is clean for her members.

"That's the biggest thing that I hear when a lady comes from somewhere else—'that other gym is so dirty!'"

"It must be because of all the men in there, sweating all over the place," Scott suggested. You can tell why he is such a big hit with the ladies.

"We have to clean every day," replied Diana incredulously. "Women sweat too!"

These components of Fit Time for Women's offerings reflect the most critical element of a product-differentiation strategy. Once you have identified your target customer, you must tweak your services in order to match the preferences of these customers as closely as possible. You could call your gym "Fit Time for Women" and hope that women would join, but they would not stay long unless they felt the gym was better than other gyms in town.

What, exactly, makes one gym "better" than other gyms? Well, that depends entirely on who you're asking—and it is why businesses pursuing a product-differentiation strategy try to target well-defined customer segments. In this case, there appear to be specific features that appeal to women that Fit Time can be sure to include as part of its gym: clean, testosterone-free, lots of fitness classes, available child care. Once Fit Time has these features, their customers will have a clear choice as to which gym they would prefer to join—that means more revenues from Fit Time's target customers.

Furthermore, in order to be efficient, a business pursuing a product differentiation strategy must be careful *not* to include services and features that do not appeal to its customers. This would represent a costly waste from the company's perspective. In the case of Diana's gym, making investments in fancy exercise equipment would not be a productive use of company funds.

"A lot of the stuff I've got is old—I've got some stuff back there that's so old that if it breaks, I can't get it fixed. You can't get the parts," Diana explained. "But the ladies don't care. A treadmill is a treadmill and as long as it moves, they're OK."

Diana's lack of investment in equipment would not be possible if she weren't targeting this particular customer segment. As she told us, her local competitors do make these costly investments on a regular basis. "The guy at the Y, he replaces his equipment every year. He gets it in and then at the end of the year gets all new stuff."

"All I can say is that some of my stuff is really old," Diana confessed.

Even though the two gyms are making different decisions regarding equipment purchases, they are both making the correct decision in terms of appealing to the preferences of their target consumers. Since the customers are different, the companies need to be different. Apple targets and attracts the hip and creative-type consumers with their stylish products; more practical corporate-types appreciate the business-friendly Microsoft platform. When customers are sorted based on their preferences, everybody wins—the customers are happier, and the businesses make more money.

This happens because the differentiation in the market helps with pricing. Suppose that all the gyms in Frankfort were more or less the same: coed facilities with reasonably good equipment, a few fitness classes, and some limited child care availability. Customers would likely view the gym experiences as indistinguishable. In such a scenario, customers would be more likely to choose their gym based on price—since they are otherwise similar, might as well go for the cheapest!

In contrast, consider how women in Fit Time's target segment make their choice, given how the gyms in Frankfort are differentiated. Some women strongly prefer Fit Time as it has the ideal characteristics from their perspective. Once a woman has found her "best-fit" gym, she is not likely to switch to another one, even if prices go up. Diana found this out when she decided to increase the monthly membership fee for her customers.

"I did a price increase the first of the year. Two dollars per month if they weren't paying the current rate. And I struggled with that," recalled Diana. She did not fully trust that her product differentiation had engendered loyalty among her customers and was worried that they would cancel instead of paying the higher price.

She needn't have worried. "I lost two. One of them was an old lady—really old, like mid-eighties—she probably did not even realize it was coming out of her bank account because her husband called me." Perhaps she could have even raised her prices more, given what a good match Fit Time for Women is with her customers' preferences.

Having a clearly defined target customer, as Diana has, provides an additional benefit in that she can bundle other value-added services to her target customers. Along with the gym, Fit Time houses several other services, which Diana enumerated.

"We have personal training. I have tanning beds. We do massage. I have a nail salon. We do spray tan. And I have a sauna. Then I also sell some products."

None of these is essential for the core gym membership, but Fit Time benefits by providing them because the "right" customers for these services are already working out at the gym. This allows the company to add to its revenue by catering to several of their target customers' needs in one location and further differentiates Fit Time. The key, as Diana said, is getting the women to experience what she has to offer.

"I have every confidence that if she comes through this door and looks at my gym, she's going to join me every time. The job is to get her through the front door."

Missoula, Montana
BANK OF MONTANA

Attract Profitable Clients;
Alienate Costly Ones

In Kentucky we saw an example of a consistent product-differentiation strategy at work, and its effects on market share and pricing. Mazzeo's Law suggests that different approaches to product differentiation will work in different situations, depending on market conditions. This was highlighted in visits we made to two community banks on consecutive days during a summertime trip through the Northwest. Though separated by only 175 miles and both recent start-ups, these two businesses were light years apart in how they positioned themselves to compete in the market for deposits.

Retail banking is an intensely competitive industry, with a small number of very large national institutions continuing to gain market share year after year. While down from over 17,000 in the mid-1980s, there are still more than 6,500 US banking organizations that engage in traditional lending and deposit-gathering activities and have limited geographic scope. According to a recent report by the FDIC, these so-called community banks held almost half of the overall loans made to small businesses. Many of the businesses we met on the road mentioned the value and importance of their community bank relationships.

Knowing about the sharp reduction in the number of community banks nationwide, we were curious to understand how brand-new banks have managed to start up in this challenging environment. In short, their success has been predicated on being different. That became clear right away as we tried to find the Bank of Montana in downtown Missoula. We figured this would be easy given that the bank is in the tallest building in town (it's nine stories—unfortunately, we did not have the honor of visiting Montana's tallest building, a twenty-story tower in Billings.) But it turned out that the bank only has a small sign on the outside of the back entrance to the building. We entered the lobby and found it to be the quietest bank ever—no ATM, deposit windows, or, for that matter, people. It didn't look like a bank at all. We were eventually able to track down the CEO, Tom Swenson, who described the origins of his alternative philosophy and approach.

"I went to graduate school for banking," Tom explained, "at the University of Washington, Pacific Coast Banking School. We took a personality test, and I was one of two guys out of 260 or so that had this 'different' personality profile. They made an example of me in class and said, 'What are you doing here? Are you sure you want to be a banker?'"

Sure enough, Tom didn't look much like your typical banker. He cut a casual figure in khaki pants and a black golf shirt. The offices were similarly informal—just 2,650 square feet of space and furniture purchased second-hand for three thousand dollars.

Paul took one look around the place and asked Tom, "Is *this* the bank?"

The spartan surroundings and casual dress were by-products of the Bank of Montana's differentiated approach. As Tom put it, they were able to start from scratch and try to avoid mistakes that were problematic for competitors (and for banks that had failed in the past).

"Basically what we saw was banks saying things like, 'If it wasn't for the 80 percent of our clients that are costing so much money, we'd be doing much better.' We thought—let's not have those 80 percent as clients."

It isn't so easy for an established bank to get rid of 80 percent of its existing customers, but Tom Swenson thought, "If you started a bank over again—started from scratch—what would you do?" He got suggestions from bankers all over the country on what they would and wouldn't do in order to avoid the most expensive customers.

"First of all—no safety deposit boxes. They cost money and take up a bunch of space. Wouldn't deal with heavily consumer-based deposits. Wouldn't have bricks and mortar."

With a clean slate, the Bank of Montana was able to establish its own value proposition to consumers without this burden. Tom articulated it as follows:

"We will pay you half a percent more on deposits if you average high deposits and if you are a low-transaction, or electronic-transaction, account. If you want heavy teller activity, lots of locations, you need to go to competitors who we know are way better than us at that."

This value proposition highlights a key part of any successful product-differentiation strategy—there will be customers who find your offering very attractive but others who will prefer what competitors have instead. In the case of the Bank of Montana, it is critical to make sure that the costly 80 percent don't choose to deposit with them. So they purposely make price and service decisions that make their bank relatively less attractive.

"Simply surveying the market—pricing up a half percent if you had more than fifty, sixty, seventy thousand, with our real target being over a hundred thousand. If you're under ten thousand, it's effectively zero interest on any account. We underpriced the lower-level accounts and overpriced the higher-level accounts."

As a result, the Bank of Montana attracted customers who deposited very large amounts into their accounts. Tom reported that their average deposit account is more than twenty times larger than that at the average bank in Missoula.

"Those same big deposit customers don't like to be nickeled-and-dimed, from my experience," Tom continued. "So, we don't charge them for faxes, minimum balances. Whatever kind of checks you want, whatever kind of leather book you want—whatever you want, just take it. It doesn't matter; because of the volume, the cost of servicing them is so low."

On the other hand, customers who have preferences for services that cost more for banks to provide will not be happy with what the Bank of Montana offers.

"People who have those high transaction accounts come in and say, 'Well your competitor has thirteen locations, they give us a backpack, they do this and that, you don't compare very well.' We say, 'Yes, we don't!'"

While Tom may appear a bit overly enthusiastic about disappointing people, his approach is critical to successful product differentiation. Too many businesses try to be all things to all people, which leads to inefficiencies. Tom knows who isn't a good customer for the Bank of Montana, and he doesn't lose sleep over not signing that customer up.

"Our competitors have all this operational staff. You have no idea what it takes to collect on bad checks. As a bank with a small customer base, we'd never make money on the fees we'd charge for bad checks anyway. Because of who our customers are, we haven't had a bad check in over four years. Not one. But we'll also call someone and say, 'Hey, you've got a mistake in your account and you need to put ten thousand dollars in there.' We want to help them avoid that situation."

Since their customers hardly ever come into the bank, Tom

doesn't need to invest anything in the facility and its upkeep. They obtained a low-cost lease by taking over office space abandoned by Morgan Stanley when it closed its office in Missoula. All together, Tom estimated that the Bank of Montana's fixed assets were worth about $175,000, compared to $6 to 10 million for a typical new bank. All of these savings allow the Bank of Montana to offer higher interest rates to its customers and still maintain a profitable operation.

Tom Swenson's success comes from recognizing that in operating a bank, you've got to think like a small business owner and not like a banker. As he put it to us in our interview, "Most people don't realize that banks are small businesses." But finally, near the end of the interview, Tom sheepishly revealed his inner banker.

"I named my second-born son Hamilton," he admitted, knowing that three economists would catch the reference to Alexander Hamilton, the first US Secretary of State of the Treasury, whose face is on the ten-dollar bill.

Post Falls, Idaho
COMMUNITY 1ST BANK

Avoid Competition by Offering
Unique Services

From Missoula, we took a three-hour drive to Coeur d'Alene, a town of about 44,000 on the Idaho panhandle. The route goes through the Lolo National Forest and over Lookout Pass and offers some of the best mountain scenery you're likely to see.

"Feel the power of that Volvo?" Scott asked as he pulled into the passing lane to blow by an eighteen-wheeler. "Aren't you glad not to be in a rental car?"

"It's great," Mike quipped sarcastically. "More power up front and waaay more Cheerios in the back. Do your kids only eat in the car?"

As Mike stared out the window at majestic purple mountains, history buffs Paul and Scott reenacted the Voyage of Discovery and argued over who got to be Lewis and who got to be Clark. "Look, everybody knows Lewis couldn't navigate his way out of a brown paper bag," Scott asserted flatly. "I'm Clark!"

"Does that mean I'm Sacagawea?" Mike asked. "I'm not sure how I feel about that."

We stopped for dinner along the way, so it was reasonably late when we finally pulled into Coeur d'Alene. Paul had, for unknown reasons, handed the task of selecting our accommodations to his teenage daughter, Lucy. Always the creative type, Lucy decided that we should try something more "interesting" and "memorable" than our usual reliable chains like Holiday Inn Express. And so it was that three tired economists arrived at the Flamingo Motel.

"Because nothing says 'Idaho' more than a flamingo!" mocked Mike, while Paul tried to defend his daughter with a feeble argument that the flamingo was Idaho's state bird.

Scott was aghast as we learned that each room was decorated with a particular theme, and that we would be choosing between the "English Garden," the "Victorian," and the "Flamingo Beach." Scrambling, Mike grabbed the key for Flamingo Beach before Scott and Paul had a chance to react, leaving them to battle over which Jane Austen movie set each would spend the night in.

Paul had his defenses prepared when we met up the next morning—great ratings on Trip Advisor! 5 stars!—but Scott was oddly good natured. Was it the bike ride he took around gorgeous Lake Coeur d'Alene that changed his mood? Or had he put a few quarters in the "Magic Fingers" bed in his room? Mike and Paul were afraid to ask.

Our first meeting of the day was with Community 1st Bank, and we were eager to compare and contrast it with the Bank of Montana. The differences emerged quickly when we met Dave Bobbitt, a white-haired extrovert in his mid-sixties who greeted us wearing a suit and tie, with his Community 1st Bank nametag pinned to the lapel. Unlike Tom Swenson, Dave fully embraces his identity as a banker—he mentioned early in our conversation that he had served a term as president of the Idaho Bankers Association and had enjoyed lengthy tenures at two larger banks before initially retiring.

"I retired on the first of July, six years ago," Dave recalled. "On the fifth of July, I got up, and my wife went to work, both my sons went to work, and I spent most of the day gazing out of the window aimlessly."

Dave's retirement lasted four whole days, but then he knew he had to get back to work. After a couple of unexciting months helping out a friend who was a contractor, he started to reacquaint himself with contacts from his days in banking. Conversations ensued, and Dave began the process of starting a new bank.

From a strategic perspective, there were two aspects of Dave's new bank that were designed to be unique and to distinguish it from the competition. The first was geographic—Dave homed in on the potential opportunity in Post Falls, Idaho, which was a smaller town of about 23,000, ten miles to the west of Coeur d'Alene.

"There had been five or six banks started in Coeur d'Alene," Dave noted, "and I'd have been just one in a long line of banks. There had been no start-ups in Post Falls—over the years a couple tried, but they couldn't raise the capital."

"We call Post Falls the 'World Headquarters' of Community 1st Bank. That's a big deal there!"

Geography can often be a critical factor, especially when transportation costs are high. Customers may prefer to buy local, and businesses can benefit from geographically based product differentiation. Being a start-up in Post Falls made Dave's bank unique on that dimension.

The other distinguishing feature of Dave's bank is right in the name—community. It is their explicit strategy to do everything possible to be community oriented and to make personal connections with individual customers.

"There's not any one thing," Dave said. "It's a lot of things we try to do as a local bank to be part of the community. Every new account that's opened gets a personal letter from me. We always have coffee and cookies in the lobby [Scott immediately perked up]—every day. We send birthday cards to every customer.

"We do a bank barbecue one Friday a month at the branch on the back deck. We do about two hundred burgers on a Friday between eleven and one. Anybody can come. We have what we call 'celebrity chefs'—the mayor of Post Falls will come out one time and the next time will be the CEO of the

Chamber of Commerce along with a city councilperson. It's gotten to be a real community event."

Dave put an emphasis on these details—at one point, he saw that there were no cookies in the lobby.

"'We don't want to have cookies every day,' they said. 'People will be hanging around the lobby all the time.' Yeah—that's what I want! I want this lobby to be like my living room in my home. I want people to come here and hang out. That's what community banking is all about."

Here, the contrast between Community 1st and the Bank of Montana could not have been more stark. While the Bank of Montana tried very hard to select for customers who were not interested in special, personalized service, Community 1st Bank put in a tremendous effort to attract these customers. As a result, while the Bank of Montana could pass the savings they achieved from having fewer services on to their customers in the form of higher interest rates on deposits, Community 1st needs to keep those rates lower to maintain its margins.

"How are you able to get people to deposit at a lower interest rate than they might get elsewhere?" Paul asked.

"Cookies," Dave responded.

We laughed, but that was basically it. Dave was able to pick up customers—and stealing market share from other existing banks was really the only way to do this, given the maturity of the industry—who were community oriented and who appreciated the additional customer service. There were some customers, indeed, who valued the personal connections enough that they were willing to accept slightly lower interest rates or higher fees on their deposit accounts. It takes some trial and error to figure out the sweet spot: How much lower a rate will customers accept? Is it OK to have burgers at the cookouts or do you need to serve prime rib? And so on. But having services that were attractive to these customers was critical to building Dave's business.

Dave benefits further because the larger banks nearby have scaled back on their community involvement. Appropriately designing your company's products or services to appeal to specific sets of customers requires thinking about the competition. If the alternatives to your product are particularly unattractive to the customers that you have targeted, then you have a greater opportunity to succeed because you are more differentiated from them.

"One large bank dropped out of the Chamber of Commerce in Post Falls when I was president," Dave recounted. "So I called the regional manager and I said, 'What's the deal—banks support chambers?' and he said, 'We've taken a policy that if our managers haven't got time to be involved, we don't need to join.' That doesn't play well with the business community in a small town like Post Falls. At another large bank, if managers want to belong to civic clubs, they have to pay for it themselves."

Product differentiation is about both what you offer *and* what the competition doesn't offer. This helps to explain how both Community 1st and the Bank of Montana could enter successfully, even though they may be polar opposites in terms of customer orientation. Both operate in a competitive environment in which large banks have developed standard approaches designed to efficiently service the mass market. As a result, these large banks don't necessarily serve customers with idiosyncratic needs (whether they are customers with high balances or those who crave deep community connections) particularly well. What Community 1st and the Bank of Montana have in common is that they both target customers that the industry serves poorly. Finding opportunities to do that is the key for small companies to find profitable niches.

Pasco, Washington
TILITE

Balance the Benefits of Customization with the Costs

Leaving Idaho, we headed southwest on US 395 through the Palouse region of eastern Washington. Rolling hills—coated with, as the song goes, amber waves of grain—stretched to the horizon, and we watched as giant combines kicked clouds of dust into the blue late-summer sky. As a result, Scott's Volvo was pretty dirty by the time we got to the Tri-Cities; the outside, that is, since Mike had long since picked every Cheerio out of the rear seat. We checked into the Cedar Inn and Suites in Kennewick, which was precisely the sort of brand-new, charmless, and completely sterile motel that Scott loves best.

The Ice Harbor Brewery, advertising good beer, fried food, and a nice setting on the Columbia River, was our dinnertime destination, and we hopped back in the car for what we thought would be a short drive to the restaurant. Shockingly, the GPS on Paul's phone malfunctioned (again!), and we ended up taking an indirect route on a narrow road through a riverside park. There, to our amazement, we encountered a massive traffic jam: ten cars at a dead stop in front of us, and nobody moving. Scott felt a pang of hunger, and immediately regretted not having grabbed an extra cookie at Community 1st Bank back in Idaho.

Mike and Paul stepped out of the car to investigate, but returned to find Scott in a full-on hunger meltdown. Accusations began to fly: Incompetent navigation! Lodging with malicious intent! Not my fault! Blame my kid! Geese!

What?

Yes, Mike and Paul had found the cause of our roadblock. A massive gaggle, led by a gander Moses parting a Red Sea of cars, was crossing the road ahead. Scott dropped his combative posture, and we quickly joined every other motorist in our traffic jam to watch and photograph. Eventually, the geese cleared and, after a beer or two, so did the air between us.

The next morning we were right back to interesting lessons in product differentiation. The previous examples in this chapter show that designing a company's products or services to appeal to a particular set of customers can yield big rewards. As the design features become more and more specific to the needs of individual consumers, products may even become customized. This was the approach adopted by TiLite, a manufacturer of "Complex Rehab Manual Wheelchairs" we visited in neighboring Pasco.

The "Ti" in TiLite refers to titanium, the strong corrosion-resistant metal that is used to make the company's wheelchairs. We spoke to Rick Forman and Josh Anderson from TiLite seated around a long table in the company's conference room, which was decorated with posters of championship wheelchair athletes. We began by asking how the company ended up on the arid plains of southeastern Washington.

"It actually goes all the way back to the Manhattan Project," Rick began, giving us a dose of American history along with the company's background.

"How much time do you have?" chimed in Josh with an eye-roll, as if he'd heard Rick tell the long version of this story before.

The Hanford Nuclear Site, which manufactured the plutonium used in the first atomic bomb, was located nearby. TiLite was a spin-off of a Swedish manufacturer of titanium tubes that were used in the plutonium manufacturing facility. As the nuclear industry waned in the 1970s and 1980s, the company searched for other applications for the metal and eventually understood its potential for wheelchairs.

"Titanium has the highest strength-to-weight ratio," Rick explained. "So you can make a much thinner-walled tube."

"There are lots of reasons why a user would prefer a titanium wheelchair," Josh went on. "The primary reason is that titanium is a vibration-dampening material. If you're spending sixteen hours in the chair every day, that comfort level is huge."

Josh spoke about the virtues of the chair from experience, as he himself is a user of the product. "I had a spinal cord injury when I was fourteen years old, so I have been using this technology for twenty-six years. I have seen it develop and I like to be a part of that development."

In addition to the strength and vibration-dampening properties, titanium has excellent shape-manipulation ability. This allows for TiLite's main user-oriented feature: customization. Manual wheelchairs are manufactured for independent users who self-propel rather than being pushed in their chairs. For manual users, mobility is enhanced substantially by having a wheelchair built specifically to the size and shape of their bodies and the challenges associated with their injuries.

"For each one of our chairs we have a very detailed order form, where we specifically ask you every measurement that we need. We define every option that is available because we make every wheelchair for a specific individual. We offer fifty different rear-wheel options—our competitors generally offer around twenty."

This comparison began to get to the heart of the differentiation advantage that customization generates for TiLite. Because of all the available configurations permitted by the shape-shifting metal—billions of potential combinations, Rick noted proudly—the more standardized products offered by competitors can't possibly be as attractive for any individual user.

"One of the measurements is seat height—front seat height and rear seat height. And then there's frame angle, the angle of that knee bend in the wheelchair. We give you four or five choices on that. Depending on what your front and rear seat height are, as you tilt one, the other changes."

"We do that; they don't," Rick summed up. "The competition doesn't, and whatever seat height you choose, your angle is going to be off—that's too bad."

"Our product is by far more custom than anyone else's," echoed Josh. "You couldn't take my chair [Josh measured more than six foot four from head to toe] if you needed one. If we just gave you my chair, it wouldn't work for you. It would be no different than your getting one of these four-hundred-dollar, low-end chairs." TiLite's chairs could be priced three times higher or more, depending on the customized options the user selects.

In hearing these descriptions of the product, there was no doubt in our minds that having a customized wheelchair would be superior from a user's perspective. For TiLite to have a successful business, however, they need to do more than just provide a better solution—the costs of providing the solution must be less than the revenue that they can generate from the customers. So a risk of a differentiation or customization strategy is that is becomes too costly to provide that unique targeted product.

"It is more expensive," Josh admitted, "but we really fine-tune our manufacturing processes so that we can limit that. Because of the initial material that we've started with—the titanium—we've streamlined our process around building custom."

Since the costs of custom manufacturing are higher, this extreme differentiation strategy will work only if appreciation of a customized product translates into users who are willing to pay higher prices. TiLite is at the top of a stratified market, and both public and private insurance providers need to be convinced that the added functionality compared to a standardized product is worth the higher price tag. When users can be more self-sufficient in their TiLite wheelchairs, that helps make the argument.

We thanked Josh and Rick as they showed us to the door and then strolled out to the car. We had seen many good examples of product-differentiation strategies, so the conversation naturally turned in that direction. "Didn't you write your PhD dissertation on product differentiation?" Paul asked Mike.

"Yeah, it was a study of motels," he replied. "I looked at rural interstate exits and examined how new entrants try to differentiate from the established players."

"Do you think your analysis can explain the Flamingo Motel?" Scott asked.

Paul rolled his eyes as Mike thought for a moment. "I can't think of a rational explanation for that."

Mazzeo's Law

Successful Product Differentiation: What It Depends On

- **Serving Your Target Customers Well:** Offering a product that has greater appeal than what competitors offer translates into true loyalty, though just for your targeted customers. Higher-wealth, low-transaction-volume consumers appreciate what the Bank of Montana offers, while consumers who want high-touch service prefer a bank like Community 1st instead.

- **Providing a Clear Alternative:** Differentiation will work best when the difference between a company's offerings and those of competitors is more pronounced. A woman who cares about working out with no men present will always choose Fit Time over the co-ed gym options—

and recall that Diana Geddes didn't lose many customers when she raised her monthly fee.

- **Customers Who Really Care:** A customer's loyalty will grow if he or she has particularly intense preferences for the product's unique features. While TiLite's customized wheelchair is better than a standard wheelchair for any user, an active, job-holding person needs more mobility and will appreciate the difference between wheelchairs more than will older, housebound users.

- **Customizing Efficiently:** The best differentiation strategies strike a balance between the revenue potential of the niche and the costs required to serve it. The Bank of Montana works hard to limit its frills so that it can make ends meet while offering higher interest rates; TiLite must keep the costs of manufacturing its customized wheelchairs in check.

CHAPTER 4

Setting Prices

We have had our share of fun and adventure on our travels. But in order to get the most out of our trips, many days involved a grueling schedule. We typically set a first meeting at 9:00 a.m.—sometimes earlier—which required an 8:00 a.m. checkout after a quick breakfast. Morning exercisers Mike and Paul would rise early, often at 6:00. Each visit with a small business took at least an hour, after which we would scramble to get to the next company, perhaps with coffee or a quick bite on the way. Five o'clock would come around before we knew it, but that didn't mean it was quittin' time. Instead of hitting a local watering hole, we'd load back into the rental car for a few hours of driving to our next town. Throw in a meal and a hotel check-in, and it was often close to midnight before we could crash.

By Thursday, our fourth straight day on the road, we were pretty beat. Scott would put everyone on edge first thing by being late (again) for our departure, leaving Mike and Paul waiting in the parking lot with packed bags and short tempers.

Scott's patience would then be tested by Paul's indecisive navigating as we steered to our first visit. And Mike's slightly acidic backseat humor would begin to cross the line from quips to insults. Paul and Scott would retaliate by mocking Mike's favorite Yankees pitcher Andy Pettitte, and things would go downhill from there. Thursday, it seemed, was Fight Day for the Roadside MBA crew.

Our first Fight Day Thursday was in Council Bluffs, Iowa. "When's our next visit, Mike?" Scott asked as we finished lunch.

"Mike?" he repeated.

"Can you wait two minutes for the Yankees highlights to finish?" Mike replied, staring at ESPN on a TV over the bar. "They were down 6–1, and in the ninth Jeter…"

"How about you put your work obligations ahead of the Yankees for once?" Scott reprimanded.

"I believe it was you who picked this dumpy sports bar. I voted for the natural foods deli."

Paul tried playing peacemaker, but Mike and Scott instead joined forces and attacked.

"Look, pal, you're the one who burned an hour getting us lost over the bridge to Nebraska," Mike said to Paul pointedly.

"We'd be at a blackjack table if it weren't for you," Scott followed. We had each won a hundred bucks the previous evening at the Harrah's casino next to the Missouri River and had planned to return over our lunch break. "You had to pick today to start asking Siri for directions?"

"The odds favor the house," Paul said, defensively. "I saved you each twenty bucks by getting lost. Plus, you got a nice tour of Omaha."

"Don't get on him for using Siri, Scott," Mike said. "Anything would be an upgrade."

It was Scott's turn to pay for lunch, and his frustration eased as he scanned the $23 check, glad he had steered Mike away from the pricey options at the natural deli. While Scott doesn't think of himself as "cheap," he will admit to the economist's euphemism of "price sensitive." And as his lunch selection illustrates, prices can be a key determinant of consumer choice. Businesses must be mindful, however, not to give away too much profit margin in order to attract customers. Setting prices is a tricky balancing act, and Mazzeo's Law suggests that the right pricing strategies will vary from business to business.

Council Bluffs, Iowa
ARNOLD TOOL

Know Your Costs

Fortunately, Fight Day in Council Bluffs was interrupted by a fantastic visit with Arnold Tool just after lunch. Even during the interview we couldn't help but show our enthusiasm for the strategies that company president Jim Hackett and his team used to successfully address some complex economic challenges. Paul summed up our sentiments as we left, telling Jim, "This was a lot of fun for us. This was really a lot of fun."

What made the visit fun was the combination of interesting economics and big tools. Arnold Tool is a machine shop that produces equipment and spare parts for factories. Their customers are large manufacturers—companies that make things from steel to soap and from batteries to bacon—whose factories use complex machinery. Arnold Tool specializes in making this machinery run more smoothly or providing replacements for parts that have failed.

"They come to us with the hard problems," Jim told us, describing his interactions with customers.

Solving these hard problems and making the parts and machinery for customers requires some big tools. It was a ninety-five-degree afternoon when we toured the un-air-conditioned building that houses Arnold Tool, but it was worth the sweat to see what was behind the process. Spread out in a long warehouse, the factory floor has more than fifteen mills, a half dozen lathes, and an assortment of presses, sanders, grinders, and ovens, machines that had been purchased over many years from a variety of sources. Pointing to one massive piece of equipment, Jim described how he'd purchased it third- or fourth-hand, and proudly asserted that it had originally been used in Germany before World War II. Employees were scattered around the machines, feeding metal in and fashioning objects of various shapes and sizes.

After the tour, Jim led us to a conference table in the cluttered back office. Jim, who wore metal rimmed-glasses on his round face and spoke softly but clearly, has been a machinist for over forty-six years. When we suggested that he might be retired in Florida the next time we visited Council Bluffs, he countered, "Nah—I'll probably be on the floor out there, doing a hobby job."

With Jim narrating, we looked through a book with color photos of projects that Arnold Tool had completed in the past.

One project was for a massive tube-drilling fixture that could make holes in 85,000-pound barrels. "They asked us if we could make a machine that could drill two thousand holes in there. All automatically, without stopping. Being younger, we all thought, 'Let's go for it.' So we did it." We were very impressed at all the creative solutions that Jim described— clearly, the smartest guy seated at the conference table was not one of the suit-wearing economists.

Arnold Tool does everything, from those big jobs to smaller ones. A customer's factory can be completely shut down if one piece of machinery fails. To get production back up quickly, customers often ask Jim to make a very specific piece of equipment in a very short time frame.

"That little board right there—that job could've been done anywhere else in town." Jim recalled, as he pointed to the picture of a smaller object that looked like a three-dimensional metal puzzle piece. "With a rotary head and a conventional mill, that job would have taken three-and-a-half days. We did it in twenty-four hours with our equipment and know-how."

From the descriptions of these jobs, we began to get the idea of how this business worked. Because of the experience of Jim and his team and Arnold Tool's history and reputation, customers come to the company with specific problems that they need solved. Paul asked whether they had salespeople, a question that drew hearty laughter.

"Salespeople? This is our sales department right here," Jim joked as he pointed to the telephone on the conference table.

So when the customers have a problem, they call Arnold Tool. But they also have other machine shops they can call. Jim told us that one large manufacturing customer had developed a list of ten quality shops (whittled down from an original list of over one hundred) that they use. So even with his impressive problem-solving history, Jim Hackett gets very little work on a "time-and-materials" basis.

"Some local customers we're time-and-materials with. Everything else we quote. For 95 percent we bid on it."

"This particular one is the Eaton Corporation," Jim said, describing a particular project's origin. "They have engineers down there, drawing these drawings up. We're well known enough with them now—they just email us this drawing. I take it in the office, I quote it, and the secretary shoots back an email with our price. That's how it starts."

While all the big machines and tools were impressive, it was this difficult task of quoting jobs that was essential to the company's success. Since each purchase order represents a custom job, Jim must look at the drawings and make a prediction about how long it will take his team to build. Jim's competitors will be doing the same thing, and the company submitting the lowest bid will get the work.

If competitors could perfectly forecast build times based on their own capabilities, the most efficient producer would win each bid. However, a company might win the bid not because it is the most efficient, but because it has underestimated the build time. This would quickly lead to trouble, as the price a company is paid for the project may not exceed the actual costs. This phenomenon—where a company is most likely to win the bid in exactly the cases where it has underestimated the cost of the job—is known as the winner's curse.

"In the past, I didn't quote high enough sometimes," Jim

reflected. But with his long experience, Jim is confident that he can now make accurate predictions very easily. "I can look at this drawing, and in thirty seconds I'll have it quoted because I've done it so often." Because Jim knows his costs, a winning bid will result in profits, rather than regrets, for Arnold Tool.

Winner's curse problems can arise even for companies that don't engage in direct competitive bidding. If a print shop, for example, posts a price for color copies, it is essentially "bidding" against all other local shops for a customer's job. The shop is most like to "win"—by capturing a large market share—exactly in the cases where it has underestimated its costs. A company with less experience must carefully account for its expected costs and think hard about business it does and does not win. It may be necessary to raise prices a bit to make sure that you are getting work because you are the most efficient, not just because you have made an inaccurate underestimate. It is possible to improve on this task quickly if you understand the consequences and keep track of the data.

Arnold Tool can fashion many kinds of complex machine parts using its big tools. But if it wants to make money, pricing is just as important as technical skill. What's true for Arnold Tool is true for all companies when determining their pricing strategy: knowing your costs is the crucial starting point.

Marietta, Georgia
MARIETTA NDT

Beyond Cost-Plus Pricing—How Much Are Your Customers Willing to Pay?

There's no better way to get the Roadside MBA team fired up than with a factory tour, especially one that features really big machines. Our enthusiasm grew as Daryle Higginbotham, wearing jeans and a button-down work shirt, led us through the facility of his company, Marietta NDT. After just a few minutes of gawking at Daryle's big toys, we began to see striking parallels with Arnold Tool.

"This is Jim Hackett's business," Scott whispered.

Not literally, of course, but the businesses did have some remarkable similarities. The "NDT" in the company's name stands for "non-destructive testing." Daryle's company manufactures testing equipment specifically designed not to damage objects while they are being tested. An example helped us to understand the value. Daryle showed off a large chamber that they had designed to test for internal cracks in newly fashioned mortar rounds. While being inspected, it is crucial—really crucial—that the mortar rounds remain intact. Marietta NDT's machine uses imaging technology (X-rays, computed tomography, eddy current, ultrasonic technology, etc.) to examine the insides of the mortar rounds for flaws.

Despite the surface similarities, Daryle's operation differed from Arnold Tool in a variety of ways. On the shop floor, the main difference was size—these tools and machinery were substantially larger. The chambers that Marietta NDT was constructing needed to be large enough to contain whatever was being inspected; some of the vaults and chambers were the size of a semitrailer. Daryle walked us through three large buildings, each as large as Jim's machine shop, with a total of over 60,000 square feet of space. Post-tour, we stepped into the conference room to ask Daryle some questions about his business.

Like Jim, Daryle has a long history of tinkering with and making machines. "My senior design project when I was in college," Daryle recalled, "was a machine that opened coins that had been wrapped in paper. It was called a 'Wrapper Snapper.' And I was going to set the world on fire selling Wrapper Snappers. But I didn't understand the market. I thought there would be a big demand for these machines and in fact there was not."

"You tried to sell the Wrapper Snapper?" Mike asked.

"And I never sold the first one" came the poignant reply.

Daryle learned quickly from that experience. Going forward, he told us, he focused on "finding people who have needs. It's like a jigsaw puzzle—you try to understand what their needs are and put together a machine to solve their problem."

Just as with Arnold Tool, Daryle needs to produce customized solutions to address his customers' testing problems. So when the conversation turned to pricing, we knew exactly the questions to ask. And sure enough, while the machines were different, the key areas of expertise were much the same. "I have an intuitive feel of how long it would take to make something. So I can price it out pretty well," Daryle said.

But, as Daryle went on, he identified a critical difference

between Marietta NDT and Arnold Tool, one that changes the pricing equation significantly.

"In the beginning I would do pretty detailed cost-estimate sheets—purchased material and estimated labor, all kinds of stuff—to come up with where I would need to be on the price of the machine. But nowadays, for the machines that we build, the price isn't necessarily based on what's it going to cost us to build it with a reasonable margin. It's based on how much the customer would be willing to pay for a machine that solved their special testing need."

The concept of "customer willingness-to-pay," which Daryle described brilliantly, can be a critical factor in pricing your products profitably. Of course, prices need to be above costs, but just adding a fixed profit margin to your cost estimate can leave a good deal of money on the table. Marietta NDT uses customer willingness-to-pay as a guide for price setting, which means Daryle can generate higher margins on some products than on others. It all depends on the customer.

"Remember that machine you saw on the floor," Daryle continued. "If we do what we want with that, it will be a three-million-dollar machine. Not because that's what it costs to make but because that's the price. We'll hit a 40 percent margin on that machine.

"Our margins vary considerably across products—it's like a scatter chart. When we bid projects, we try to bid at 20 percent margin. But there will be those that hit 40 percent and those where we'll squeak just to break even," Daryle said.

In order to price based on willingness-to-pay, two requirements must be met. First, the market in which you operate cannot be *too* competitive—otherwise, another company can attract the customer by offering to sell at a lower price. For Marietta NDT, their unique abilities put them in a category where competition isn't the decisive factor. "We are fortunate to be in a pretty specialized market," Daryle confirmed. "People seek us out quite often. There are some things that are openly competitive bids, but when you do a good job and it's something that not too many other people can do, they stick with you."

The second requirement is that you must have some way of assessing the customer's willingness-to-pay. Unfortunately, this is not something a customer is likely to share enthusiastically; after all, if you think a customer's willingness-to-pay is ten dollars and it is actually fifteen dollars, the customer will end up with a discount relative to what they would have been willing to pay. To make such assessments, effective pricing managers engage with the customer and try to get inside the customer's mind to understand the true value of the product.

To do this, Daryle listens hard for clues in conversation. "Many times on some of the bigger projects they will have put together some initial funding requests that they've got budgets for. So you ask them—sometimes they'll tell you and sometimes they won't. You go, 'Is this a funded project?' and if they say yes, you say, 'Well, how much do you have in the budget?'"

At Arnold Tool, Jim Hackett is occasionally able to price in this manner—to those for whom Jim Hackett's shop was far superior to the alternatives—but not too often. These were the 5 percent of jobs that Jim didn't have to quote. One of his local customers, a factory that produced bacon and other products for frozen food companies, had Italian machinery in their factory but found that it was often difficult to get spare parts in a timely fashion. Rather than wait on Italy when production was shut down, they just gave the work to Arnold Tool. This meant Jim didn't have to bid against competitors, and could price based on willingness-to-pay. To assess willingness-to-pay, Jim thinks hard about how long his customer's plant will be shut down without his parts.

To price effectively in such a situation, it is usually a good idea to start with a high price based on what you think your product is worth to the customer. The customer will always try to bargain down from a high price that you suggest, but they aren't going to offer to pay you a higher price just because you've underestimated their willingness-to-pay! If you are offering something they need and there isn't a suitable alternative offered by a competitor, you'll have a good chance to maintain that high price.

Smyrna, Georgia
DOGMA DOG CARE

Segment the Market Based on Price Sensitivity

We left Marietta NDT on a factory-tour high but quickly crashed back to earth. It was a Thursday, after all, and it was hard to say which of the three of us was most exasperated with the other two. Adding to our troubles was the unpleasant fact of being in a major metroplex; our travels through rural America had spared us, mostly, from the dense traffic of spots like suburban Atlanta. The combination of lack of sleep and the late spring heat was making Mike a tad carsick in the backseat.

Up front, meanwhile, a battle raged over how to get to our next destination. "We could take State Road 280," Paul mused. "That would be more interesting than the interstate, but there might be a lot of stop lights. Oh, but the freeway was jammed earlier this morning. What time do you think rush hour ends here?"

"Just tell me where to turn," Scott demanded impatiently. "We only have twenty-five minutes."

"Take the freeway!" Mike yelled from the back, getting more and more nauseated from all the starting and stopping.

"OK—the freeway," Paul said, clicking data into his phone. "Uhhhh, turn around and go back about half a mile…"

"We've passed it!?! I can't make a U-turn here. Find the 280 route!"

After some twenty minutes of missed turns and angry barbs, we were hopelessly lost and boiling mad. Finally, Mike pointed to a large billboard with a jumping dog and an arrow labeled "TURN HERE." Scott—finding at last a safe place for a U-turn—drove down the side road as the sign directed and we arrived.

We found a typical suburban industrial park with a series of connected low buildings. Inside the main entrance, we were rewarded: a bright retail space with concrete floors and—a golden retriever to greet us! Three or four dogs soon milled about us, giving each of us a furry friend to pet. After a few minutes, our slacks were covered with just-shedded fur, but our moods had improved considerably. Walking past a row of shelves displaying dog toys and designer food, we stopped at the front desk to ask for Robin Crawford, the owner of Dogma Dog Care.

Robin, an African American in her mid-fifties with short hair, greeted us with a big smile and firm handshakes. With the promise of more dogs, she coaxed us into taking a tour of the facility. From the retail and intake area in the front, we walked back through a veritable maze—passing by rooms of different shapes and sizes. There was a large open room with some dogs playing together and some resting by themselves. A different area had a couple dozen crates on shelves where dogs would spend the night. We rounded a corner into a hallway with a series of doors, each painted with different designs. These were themed suites where some dog owners liked to board their best friends.

Our tour ended in Robin's office, where she described how she came to own a doggie-day-care business. A former human resources professional, Robin had built a successful career with a six-figure income overseeing diversity programs for large corporations like IBM, Coca-Cola Enterprises, and WellPoint Health Networks. Her skills and expertise, however, were not sufficient to avoid being laid off as each of these companies downsized. Exhausted by the corporate world, she decided to do something completely different.

"I always had a love of dogs," Robin explained, and after being put through these corporate upheavals, she needed a change. "I'd had it—mentally, spiritually, financially. I wanted to do what I loved. I'd been toying with this idea for years, but I just didn't have the courage. How do you give up the security of a successful career and go out into the abyss, the unknown?"

Robin's challenges in the corporate world ultimately gave her the push that she needed to set out as a business owner.

But the philosophies that guided her work as a diversity officer continue to guide how she operates a business that, on the surface, is quite different.

"What I am trying to do here is the same sort of thing. I take pit bulls—because I don't believe that every pit bull is bad. I believe you judge a pit bull on its character. We do a temperament test on every dog, whether it's a poodle or a pit bull. If they can get along with other dogs, with a female handler or a male handler, if they have a gentle personality—then the pit bull is allowed to come. People appreciate that I am not narrow in my approach."

"I never thought of diversity applying to pit bulls before," Paul joked. But the idea struck a chord with Mike, who had once owned a pit-bull mix and often felt judged by other dog owners.

Robin uses a similar approach in providing options for her customers—recognizing that different people might have different preferences for their dog's accommodations while at Dogma. "I don't just have caged boarding or open boarding alone," Robin described. "I offer all of it. My philosophy is to offer a diverse set of things—a diverse set of products and services."

The strategies Robin uses to price her diverse offerings are rooted in one of the most important concepts that economists use to think about pricing. A simple but important point is that customers are more likely to buy a particular product if the price of that product is lower. This sets up a clear trade-off between margin and volume. Higher prices mean higher margin and lower quantity; lower prices will increase your quantity but at the cost of a lower margin. Balancing this trade-off requires understanding how sensitive your customers are to price. If customers are sensitive to price, then pushing for a higher margin will cost you a lot of volume. Conversely, if customers are not price sensitive, then you can raise prices without losing a lot of customers.

Understanding the drivers of consumer price sensitivity is therefore crucial for effective pricing, and there are two primary considerations. The first involves customer preferences. If customers really like the product or service you offer, they are apt to stick with you if you raise your price. The second consideration is competition. If customers have a reasonable alternative to what you are selling, you will be more vulnerable to losing sales if you raise your price.

For many businesses, price sensitivity varies considerably from one customer to another because preferences and competition can affect different customers in different ways. Geography is often a critical consideration impacting both preferences and competition: Robin reported that her customers often drop dogs off on their morning commute and pick them up on the way home after work. Depending on where a customer lives, Dogma could be right on the way or require a substantial detour. Depending on where a customer works, Dogma could be the only convenient option, or there could be several.

It would be very good for Robin's business if she could charge different prices to these different customer groups, reflecting the differences in price sensitivity. By charging low prices to the price-sensitive consumers, she can draw in customers who otherwise would go elsewhere. If she can, at the same time, charge high prices to the price-insensitive customers, she can maintain strong margins on this group. To execute such a pricing strategy, a business needs to be able to assess the price sensitivity of individual customers, segment the market into groups of customers whose price sensitivities are similar, and come up with a way to charge different prices to the different groups. Robin has an opportunity to do this through her advertising strategy.

"Where I get the biggest bang for my buck is in the small, local mags. Even if it's the subdivision magazines, a lot of them will contract out for something that's professionally done. Not only is it more affordable, but it targets — really pinpoints — local communities I need to get into."

Scott was incredulous, "The subdivisions have magazines?"

"It's perfect," Robin continued. "I can afford to buy a full-page ad and say, for example, if you live in Vining Estates bring in this ad and get your first day free or 20 percent off your boarding stay."

Using this method, Robin could develop a very specific pricing strategy. She could select particular subdivisions where the locations are a bit more remote or the geography suggests there will be more competition and offer consumers there lower prices through the coupons in their newsletters. For customers who live in subdivisions that are directly adjacent to Dogma's facility, there would be no benefit from distributing the coupons. Selective couponing connects prices to consumers' price sensitivity (without explicitly charging based on a customer's address, which would seem inherently unfair and discriminatory).

Savvy businesses execute this approach to pricing all the

time. The pervasive practice of offering student discounts—think of restaurants and movie theaters near college campuses—is one example. Students are often cash-strapped, which means they tend to be price sensitive, shopping around to find things cheap. College-issued IDs provide a convenient means for businesses to segment; that is, to separate the starving students from the recently graduated (and, hopefully, employed).

The various options for dog boarding at Dogma Dog Care provide another opportunity to segment customers based on their price sensitivity. Having areas for open and caged boarding as well as luxury suites is really just the canine equivalent of an airplane's first-class, business, and coach sections. It is important to have an option available for customers who are willing to pay more (or willing to pay to avoid the lowest class of service). In fact, it is often in the company's best interest to reduce the attractiveness of the lowest-quality service offerings—to encourage customers to choose a higher-quality, higher-priced alternative.

The pricing for the various options should also be influenced by the presence of alternatives since this will also affect price sensitivity. Dogma's higher-end options are unique in the market, but there are several facilities that offer caged boarding. Robin needs to have pricing comparable to theirs if she wants to keep her cages full.

"Sometimes, even if I have to cut my price by fifty cents to beat PetSmart, I will," Robin admitted. "For some customers, that seems to mean a lot."

Hattiesburg, Mississippi
MISSISSIPPI MUSIC

Put Related Products Together and Price the Bundle

We encountered a different type of pricing challenge when we visited the corporate offices of Mississippi Music—a chain with four retail stores located throughout the southern half of the state. As the name implies, the company specializes in selling instruments, electronics, and other items related to the creation of music. A mural painted on the company's low-rise brick office building celebrates the rich music history of the state. Stopping to admire the artwork on our way in, we identified Jimmy Buffett, who attended Hattiesburg's Southern Mississippi University, as well as rock-and-roll pioneer Jerry Lee Lewis.

The mural also depicted two marching band members, which offered a significant clue as to the nature of the business. We chatted briefly with the friendly receptionist and waited in a wood-paneled conference room for the company president, Rosi Johnson. A trim woman with sparkling blue eyes, Rosi wore a black-and-white patterned sweater with large buttons. Rosi has been with the company for forty years, having been hired out of college by the company's founder—the father of her boyfriend, Dex, who had just joined the navy.

"We weren't too serious at the time—we hadn't talked about getting married or anything," Rosi recalled with a laugh in her deep Mississippi drawl. "But his mom and dad were keeping up with me. His father called me right before I graduated college and said, 'I've got a proposition for you. I want you to think about coming to work for Mississippi Music.'"

Knowing a good woman when he saw one, Dex's father convinced Rosi to join the company in the business office and help out with computerizing the company's processes.

"So I joined the company in 1973 and at the end of 1973, Dex asked me to marry him. That's history!"

"That's better than Internet dating!" Paul interjected, clearly focused on his upcoming weekend back in California.

As we talked more about the company, we learned that about two-thirds of its business came from students in school bands and orchestras. Consequently, the company devotes considerable resources to generate and support these customers. Rosi is the vice president of the National Association of School Music Dealers, and the company regularly funds clinics for school band directors. Several sales representatives focus on the school band business, promoting their products to the parents of children who are interested in joining the band. Given their importance to the success of the business, Rosi herself attends many of these sessions.

In order to convert interested students into revenue from instrument sales, Mississippi Music has to think carefully about pricing. Instrument manufacturers typically specify a MAP—minimum advertised price—that limits flexibility on pricing the instrument itself. But Rosi can add offerings, creating a bundle that makes the instrument more attractive to purchase.

The first has to do with the overall cost of the instrument. Depending on the quality of the brand and the size of the instrument (Encourage your kid to try the flute rather than the tuba!), even a basic introductory model could easily run a parent several hundred dollars. Given the tight budgets of many families, an expense of this size would be problematic. This problem is exacerbated by the fact that, as an overeducated economist would say, consumers have uncertainty about their own preferences. Rosi put it more directly:

"The student might not like band."

This uncertainty creates a big problem, especially since the instruments are so expensive. If parents hesitate to have the students try out the band due to the uncertainty and the expense, Mississippi Music is going to have a very difficult time selling many instruments.

Mississippi Music addresses this by offering potential customers a "rent-to-own" payment arrangement—along with the instruments they sell. Indeed, we learned that state law requires the company to set up a separate financing division in order to offer this bundled service. Parents pay a monthly fee to have their child use the instrument, and a portion of each month's payment can be applied to the sale price. After a certain number of months of making payments, the would-be musician owns the instrument.

The financing contract also contains return privileges. Consider a fourth-grader who expresses some interest in playing the trumpet. If he or she takes lessons for a while but then gets bored, the instrument can be returned and the remaining payments cancelled. On the other hand, if your child likes band a lot and is on the way to being the next Wynton Marsalis, the equity built up can be transferred to a higher-quality instrument more suitable for high school bands.

Mississippi Music offers another add-on to make the bundle of services more attractive. For an additional small monthly fee a parent can buy maintenance-and-replacement service in case their child's trombone, say, gets run over by a bus.

"I bet that actually happens a lot with school instruments," Mike joked.

"It does happen—a child sets it down on the ground and SMASH!!" Rosi replied. "We actually have some crushed instruments that we show when we go to band parent-night meetings."

"This used to be a saxophone...," Scott imagined the visual display.

"That's right," Rosi picked up, "and for this nominal fee you have coverage!"

Mississippi Music bundles the maintenance-and-replacement contract with the instrument rental based on the fact that, if they are going to buy the instrument, parents are likely very interested in protection from busses (or other potential accidents). Having the financing arrangement in the bundle effectively increases the willingness-to-pay for instruments, which is essential since the MAP policy prevents discounting to attract customers. Businesses should be on the lookout for these situations in which the purchase of one product affects the attractiveness of a related one to consumers. Bundling these "complementary goods" together can generate opportunities for additional sales and revenues.

We thanked Rosi for her hospitality and strode out to the car. "Can we stop at one of Rosi's stores?" Paul asked. "I want to check out the baby grands and play my new piece." Paul had been taking piano lessons for a few months and even boldly referred to himself as a "piano player" during our discussion with Rosi.

"Um...I don't think...We've got no time for that," Scott stammered.

"I think Rosi said the store was closing early today," Mike added. "Isn't it Groundhog Day?"

"It's jealousy like this that broke up the Beatles, you know," Paul said, shaking his head.

Mazzeo's Law

Setting the Right Price: What It Depends On

- **Knowing Your Costs:** A company needs to make positive margins on the products and services that it sells, so the right price for anything must be greater than its cost to produce. When there is uncertainty about costs, as is the case for Arnold Tool, being able to predict those costs better than competitors do is critical in order to avoid the winner's curse.

- **Customers' Willingness-to-Pay:** Customers' willingness-to-pay will be higher in situations where they have strong preferences for the product. Since alternatives to what Marietta NDT can build are limited, they listen to clues about their customers' willingness-to-pay and can charge prices higher than a margin plus their costs.

- **Segmenting Your Customers:** Companies can expand their market by having a lower-priced option available for their most price-sensitive consumers and a higher-priced option for customers who want extras or will choose you no matter what. Dogma Dog Care charges high prices for luxury suites but can offer coupons to customers who could easily choose a different dog care company.

- **Finding Opportunities to Bundle:** Willingness-to-pay for one product can often be enhanced by selling it in combination with other, related products. Mississippi Music's rent-to-own financing and their maintenance-and-replacement contract made parents more likely to buy an instrument for their aspiring young musician.

CHAPTER 5

Managing Your Brand

One of our hobbies while cruising from town to town was watching for interesting marketing efforts on billboards or other signage. Everybody's got something to sell, which means that there's a bit of economics behind every roadside communication. A sign in front of a business on the same block as Graceland—"The Foot Specialists / Est 1970 / Drs Gold and Cook / Podiatrists"—triggered much speculation about why this business is still there when most everything else within two miles is touristy fast food, a cheap motel, or a Vegas-Elvis trinket shop. Other signs made us think that recently divorced guys probably weren't the target demographic; "Your wife is HOT! Buy her an ICEE!" screamed a convenience store sandwich board in Council Bluffs. Still others, like this one in Hickory, North Carolina, just left us scratching our heads: "Night Secrets / The Ultimate Fantasy Store / Drive Thru."

But few signs had as large an impact on our choices as this one, which we saw in North Carolina: "James K. Polk Memorial, Exit 65B."

"Scott, take this exit," Paul said excitedly.

"But you just said the mini-golf is up ahead three miles," said Mike.

The three of us had flown into Charlotte, and we were, per our usual Sunday, playing tourist. A seventy-two-hole mini-golf tournament, we had decided, was the only fair way to determine who was paying for dinner.

"Nope. Change of plans. There's a Polk Memorial!" Paul exclaimed.

Scott took the exit, which dumped us onto Polk Street in the small suburban town of Pineville. Paul, it turns out, is a bit of a fanboy when it comes to our eleventh president, and he quickly began a hagiographic recounting of the Polk Golden Years. "He cut tariffs, settled the Oregon boundary dispute with the British, and acquired the entire American Southwest. All in just one term. You know, Utah would still be part of Mexico if it weren't for Polk."

Scott shrugged, thinking it might be easier to get a *cerveza* if Mexico were still running the place.

We wound south through town, coming eventually to the James K. Polk State Historic Site, which is a wooded twenty-acre patch tucked between Little Sugar Creek and an Ashley Furniture Homestore. We rolled to a stop in the deserted parking lot, and Paul jumped out to explore.

Mike, exasperated, reached for his headphones. "I'm staying here and streaming the Yankees game. Jeter has 2,965 hits."

Scott stepped out into the early afternoon sunshine, stretched his legs, and then wandered over to Paul, who had already surveyed the grounds. "This is where Polk was born," Paul said, "but it's a total rip-off."

"A rip-off? We didn't pay anything," Scott replied.

Ignoring him, Paul continued. "First off, this is land that Polk's parents once owned, but these buildings are reconstructions. If you go to Monticello, you get the real deal."

"Second, the visitor center and museum are closed Sunday."

Scott and Paul examined the outsides of locked late-eighteenth-century replica buildings for ten minutes and then walked back to the rental car. Figuring there was still time for fifty-four holes, we piled in and drove to our mini-golf destination. Paul, usually our best player, was way off his game and fell into third place with a quadruple bogey on the back-nine windmill.

Business owners everywhere strive to build demand and influence consumer choice, much as the highway sign in North Carolina caused us to re-arrange our day to visit the Polk birthplace. We learned, through our journeys, that efforts to "get the message out" and "manage our brand" take up a large share-of-mind for many small business owners. It can, however, be confusing to listen to these stories because people use the word "brand" to mean so many different things. Mazzeo's Law suggests that it's important to think through what problem you're trying to solve with your branding efforts. Different products often require different approaches to marketing and branding. In this chapter, we examine various facets of this difficult problem.

Hickory, North Carolina
BLIND SQUIRREL DIGITAL

Use Brand When Customers Don't Have Direct Experience

The next morning we woke to overcast skies and a hint of spring rain and found our way to Blind Squirrel Digital. Located just a block off Main Street in Hickory, North Carolina, the business started in 2009 as a partnership between Mike Neely, a Hollywood 3D animation veteran, and Jeremy Cooper, whose background includes a stint doing animation and programming for the video-game maker Electronic Arts. Entering a glass storefront, we found ourselves in a narrow space that felt like a theater lobby, complete with a few old movie posters. Mike N. and Jeremy, dressed just barely on the casual side of the casual/sloppy line, stepped from the back to say hello and led us through curtains to an open room that was filled with massive computer workstations. Personable, funny, and thirty-something, Mike N. and Jeremy have a solid rapport and build easily on each other's thoughts in conversation. "I'm ADD and he's OCD, so it's a really nice partnership," Mike N. said when describing their working relationship.

Blind Squirrel's main capability is 3D computer animation, and they apply this skill in both of the founders' home industries: movies and video games. In the movie business, they do freelance pre-visualization work for special-effects blockbusters while, on the video game side, they create iOS games for Apple's App Store. We asked about each in turn.

"Last summer," Mike N. began, "we worked on *Rise of the Planet of the Apes*, starring James Franco. We do pre-visualization, which is building an animated model of what shots they're going to need when they start production and making sure it's feasible to get them. We get storyboards and 3D models of set pieces, build models of other assets, and make sure everything's to scale. Then we add in a virtual camera rig, so they can know whether this camera's going to actually fit in this space. For example, there's a kitchen scene and a spiral staircase and the monkey has to go up, and the camera has to get *this* shot, so the special effects guys can get the monkey right in post-production."

"So pre-visualization isn't something you see when you go watch the movie?" Paul asked.

"No," Jeremy replied. "We help with the planning part. Pre-production and production."

"If you can't see it, what makes somebody good at it?" Scott asked. "What does a good pre-vis team do?"

Mike N. thought for a second. "One thing is speed. For the *Apes* project, they were already behind when we came on; it was under the gun and had to be fast. Trust is another thing. I once got a call from Sony trying to figure out who was posting 3D assets from *Spiderman 3* on the Internet. They eventually found the guy, and he won't be working in the industry anytime soon. And you have to be good to work with—you need to be happy in the twelfth hour of a twelve-hour day. Reputation really matters in this business."

"And when you're not making movies?"

"We do games," Mike N. replied. "Principally on iOS, so these are iPhone and iPad. We have two games on the App

Store now, and two more in the works for release at the end of this month."

"How does the sales and marketing work?" Scott asked.

"We try to push word-of-mouth through Facebook and Twitter, and we made a video on YouTube for one," Jeremy replied.

"If you can get the staff at Apple to play your game," Mike N. added, "that's big. People follow their lists of new and no-table like crazy. And you can pay somebody to review your game—you pay thirty-five dollars and they'll publish an honest review. You might get baked or you might get kudos."

While movie pre-vis and mobile-phone video games would seem, at first glance, to be quite different, they share one important characteristic: Both are examples of experience goods. Experience goods are products for which the customer has a difficult time assessing the quality before purchase. A movie producer looking for a pre-vis provider cares, according to Mike N. and Jeremy, about speed, trustworthiness, and attitude. However, it would be quite difficult for a producer to assess—prior to signing a contract—whether an unfamiliar pre-vis operation can meet these performance standards. Similarly, for video games, consumers want a new game that is fun and challenging, but they need to purchase and play the game to see if it passes the test. In both cases customers face an information problem: They won't know exactly what they've bought until the deal's already done.

In cases like this, consumers often find it useful to listen to the experiences of other, similar users, and infer from these experiences whether they too might value the product. Hence, for companies that sell experience goods, managing their brand means managing the information available to potential customers about the hard-to-assess characteristics of their offerings. For experience goods, brand is a reputation that's directly rooted in the experiences of others.

Blind Squirrel illustrates two ways in which these reputations can develop. In the movie business, Blind Squirrel relies on word-of-mouth within the Hollywood community to try to get the next film. Movie people talk, and it's important for Blind Squirrel to manage what gets said about them. They do this first by doing a good job to earn strong recommendations, but second by constantly reminding their past customers—via Skype, email, and chat, since Mike N. and Jeremy can't "do lunch" in LA—of their past successes.

In the games market, experience goods create a business opportunity for third-party "raters" to try to fill the information gaps facing potential customers. Information intermediaries can come in different forms, from the thirty-five-dollar-a-review site that Mike N. mentioned to Yelp and TripAdvisor (which we frequently used to get recommendations from other travelers about experience goods like motels and restaurants). Managing a brand in an environment like this means finding ways to access the most trustworthy and influential third-party raters, and this means the competition isn't so much for the customers directly, but rather for the attention of the raters. This, however, can be a catch-22. If raters can be lobbied or cajoled into providing good ratings, then consumers will lose confidence in the quality of the information provided. Any rater who can be effectively lobbied by Blind Squirrel probably isn't one that Blind Squirrel is interested in being endorsed by.

Jeremy explained that, given this rater credibility problem, a passive approach may be best: "You want it to go viral and let it take care of itself. You have to have a really good game, and then IGN has to pick it up and review it, which then gets GameStop to review it. That's how it propagates."

Johnson City, Tennessee
MORRIS-BAKER FUNERAL HOME AND CREMATION SERVICES

Advertise More When Consumers Don't Comparison Shop

After wrapping up our day in Hickory, we decided to take the scenic route through the mountains to Johnson City, Tennessee. Mist turned to drizzle as we climbed past the town of Boone, North Carolina, however, and we ended up with a white-knuckle drive on a blue highway through a gray fog. Corkscrewing through the Cherokee National Forest on US 321, we caught occasional glimpses of Watauga Lake, a Tennessee Valley Authority project that was completed in 1948.

"This would be pretty if it weren't for the clouds," Mike said from the back seat. "What mountains are these?"

"These are the Blue Ridge Mountains," Scott said through gritted teeth, concentrating on the winding road.

"No way," Paul scoffed. "Those are in West Virginia."

"You're lecturing me about geography based on what you learned in a John Denver song?" Scott challenged.

"Yes, I am," Paul replied. "I really need to spend the night in West Virginia sometime. When are we going there?"

The next day we visited Morris-Baker Funeral Home and Cremation Services, a spacious and well-maintained facility about ten minutes north of downtown Johnson City, and chatted with owner Preston McKee. Preston's grandfather, Carson Baker, purchased the business from Forrest Morris in 1966. In his thirties and soft-spoken, with a serious demeanor befitting his profession, Preston described growing up in the business. "I remember lying in my bed when I was thirteen, thinking about what kind of employer I was going to be."

Our conversation began with a discussion of recent trends in the funeral industry. Consolidation, Preston said, has been a big story in recent decades, and this has led to problems for Morris-Baker. "We're not affiliated with a cemetery," he began. "So one of our competitive challenges comes from Monte Vista Cemetery just a quarter mile up the road. It was purchased by a national conglomerate, and their service is so poor. If a customer had a bad experience there, they'd sometimes try another cemetery like Washington County Memory Gardens. But that cemetery has their own funeral home, so we'd lose a customer even if we did a good job.

"There are also issues as people transition to cremation," he continued. "Our cremation revenue is about half of our revenue from traditional burial, but the difficulty of the work is the same. We were in the wilderness on how to serve that market for a while. We present families a traditional option with the body present for a service, a contemporary option where the urn is present for a service, and then another option without a formal ceremony."

"How do people make the decision about which funeral home to use?" Paul asked.

Preston thought for a moment and then described some of the market research from the industry. "On a pre-need basis—people who are looking around for help planning in advance of need—three customers out of four don't consider multiple firms. Only one out of four visits multiple funeral homes."

"So if you convert three out of four," Mike noted, "then it seems like a big part of the marketing challenge would be getting people to come to you as the first option. What things do you do to get people to start here?"

"My mom, who did a lot of our home visiting after the death, noticed that no matter what the socioeconomic level, all the homes around here have two La-Z-Boy recliners directly across from a big-screen TV. So we're really focused on television."

Preston's description of consumer shopping behavior in this market—limited search prior to purchase—fits the definition of a *search good*. In contrast to experience goods, where product quality can be assessed only after consumption, search goods are those for which customers can, by making a somewhat costly investment of their own time and energy, assess many of the relevant characteristics of the product prior to making a purchase. Much as one would test-drive a car, a customer shopping for a funeral home on a pre-need basis can, for example, get to know the funeral director, and examine the chapel, caskets, and urns prior to making a purchase decision. Importantly, this search is costly—probably in part because funeral planning is no one's favorite activity—so customers engage in limited search. Most choose not to explore all their possible options.

Paul asked, "And where are you doing most of your TV advertising?"

"Right in the middle of *Deadliest Catch*," Preston said, so deadpan that we didn't laugh just in case he might be serious.

Preston gave us a look, laughed, and said, "That's a joke."

We glanced sideways at each other, embarrassed, and laughed with him.

He continued. "I don't ever see our commercials on air, since they're after that older demographic. Principally it's the female spouse who makes the decision, so we want to build a strong brand awareness with her."

For companies that sell search goods, managing their brand means getting at or near the top of a customer's mental list of searchable vendors. Increasing brand awareness by simply getting your name out there and repeating it—even if you don't say much else—can be an effective strategy in markets for search goods. In some cases, brand awareness campaigns are designed simply to catch the attention of a customer and then stick in his or her mind; think, for example, of the late-night-TV antics of a used-car salesman, or a catchy jingle one might hear on the radio. While antics or jingles would clearly be inappropriate for Morris-Baker, Preston must find the right decision maker, and get his name in front of her.

While Morris-Baker works hard to influence customer search through advertising, this isn't the only aspect of the company's brand that matters. Some customers, Preston says, ask friends and neighbors for recommendations about which local funeral homes are known to provide superior service. The funeral home business combines elements of search good and experience good, so Preston must think about both brand awareness (to influence search) and brand word-of-mouth reputation (to provide information about service quality).

Liberal, Kansas
COLLINS DIAMONDS

Develop Persuasive Branding for Occasional or Aspirational Purchases

While Preston McKee works to influence customers to come to *his* funeral home, he doesn't need to convince you to consider buying funeral services; if you don't need him now, you'll need him later. Things are a bit different for Audie Bartel, the owner of Collins Diamonds in Liberal, Kansas. Audie's store, white with a huge "Collins Diamonds" sign on the roof, is located on the not-very-happening main street (Kansas Avenue) of Liberal. While a few storefronts along Kansas Ave were operating on the wintry day we visited, many of Audie's neighbors were "For Rent" and "Lease This Space."

We walked into the showroom, which was dark with numerous but sparsely stocked display cases and TVs tuned to ESPN, and surveyed the merchandise while a salesperson summoned the owner. Audie bounced out from the back room and greeted us. Around sixty with a receding hairline and a big smile, Audie wore a maroon shirt, a gold tie, and a white suit. It was after Labor Day—or maybe before, since the Christmas season had just passed—but it was immediately clear that Audie was just the kind of guy to break fashion rules and get away with it.

Audie started as a traveling salesman in the business and spent much of the 1970s driving from town to town with half a million in inventory in his trunk. Collins Diamonds was one of his accounts, and Audie, with a partner, bought the store in 1981. He now co-owns it with his wife, Karla.

He has in recent years changed his product-market positioning considerably. "One of my original problems was too much inventory, and I couldn't figure out a way to turn it. So I've been doing what I call moving upstream. My average retail sale averaged around $750 back in 2004, and in '08 I think I had that up to $6,500. We are selling fewer pieces but better things."

To facilitate up-market purchases, Audie has worked closely with a local bank to ease financing. "I've got a bank I'm working with now where I can offer customers no-interest, no-down-payment financing for two years. I pay the interest to the bank up front, but it's great; I get paid right away, and the customer gets instant gratification."

"Who's on the hook if the customer doesn't pay?" Paul asked.

"The bank sends a couple of notices, and then they'll pass it back to us," Audie said. "There's really no risk for the bank."

Karla, Audie's wife and business partner, jumped in. "In thirteen years, we've probably only had two. And both times we got the piece back."

Audie nodded. "They brought the piece back and apologized. This is different from a car. It's something personal, and customers want to maintain a relationship with us for when their circumstances change."

Audie's marketing strategy ties in with his upstream reorientation and the personal nature of jewelry-purchase decisions. "Ours is an emotion-based advertising," he explained. "A few years ago we ran a radio ad about a guy whose dream car was a black Corvette. We said, 'It will be a lot easier for you to get that car if you'll buy her a two-carat diamond.'"

Scott nodded and took notes on the off chance that someone was willing to marry him again.

"A couple months after the campaign ended," Audie continued, "I was at a football game, and a customer tapped me on the shoulder. She had this big smile and said 'You know that Corvette commercial of yours? Turns out it applies to guns too!'"

Whereas Morris-Baker advertises to be the first stop when a customer decides to start shopping for a funeral home, Collins Diamonds hopes to motivate the up-market jewelry customer to start shopping in the first place. No one *needs* a $6,500 piece of jewelry, so Audie's message provides a reminder to the customer of the special place that jewelry has in the heart of a loving spouse. In so doing, Audie hopes to turn an aspirational customer into an actual customer, and an occasional customer into a regular.

This branding strategy also fits well with Audie's up-market positioning. To see why, consider how his branding and advertising choices might be different if he were selling lower-priced engagement rings targeted at young couples. Jewelers selling engagement rings don't have to motivate the purchase decision; that decision is motivated instead by young love. If Audie's business were primarily engagement rings, he'd want to build brand awareness so he'd be the first stop of every groom-to-be; that is, he'd want to behave more like Morris-Baker.

(And, yes, you read that right: Three divorced men just compared purveyors of engagement rings to providers of funeral services.)

Notably, Audie's Corvette campaign will tend to build demand for high-end jewelry generally, rather than demand for his store in particular. That is, he's answering a "Why jewelry?"

question, not "Why Collins Diamonds?" Persuasive marketing can drive customers to other, similar jewelers, which means a company must have sufficiently large market share in order for these investments to pay off. Audie's market, in tiny Liberal, is not crowded with competitors in the high-end jewelry space, so there is little risk that he is spending money to drive customers to his competitors.

Spartanburg, South Carolina
PRICES' STORE FOR MEN

Build Brand Image When Consumers Can Bond with Your Product

In other cases, the marketing of a good or service can be part of the value the purchaser receives when consuming it. The creation of, for example, a compelling story of a business or image around a product can itself be part of the product's allure. We saw a wonderful example of this on Main Street in downtown Spartanburg, South Carolina, where we visited Prices' Store for Men.

Harry Price, the third-generation proprietor, began our meeting with a proud description of the store's founding. "It was 1903—just thirty-eight years after the Civil War—and my grandfather came down from New York. He was a Yankee and he was Jewish, and this town welcomed him with open arms. We have deep roots here."

Harry then discussed how the business has changed since he took over from his father in the 1990s. "As menswear has shifted away from tailored clothing, our inventory has changed accordingly. Sportswear now predominates, as our teenage/college-age target market has grown. During the recent recession, that thirty- to fifty-five-year-old customer hibernated, and he's finally re-emerging."

"That's us!" Mike said, as Paul and Scott quickly inventoried their outfits to see if we might need Harry's help.

One key, Harry says, for attracting the high school and college students—Wofford College is less than a mile away and has had an historic connection with his store—is carrying young men's lines. But he's no Abercrombie knockoff, choosing instead to emphasize regional menswear lines, "things that are predominantly Southern and traditional."

"What's an example?" Paul asked.

Pointing to displays of mostly preppie-style clothes, Harry made a list of different brands: "Southern Tide is from Greenville, Southern Proper from Atlanta, Peter Millar is from North Carolina, Mountain Khaki too. Our market has really responded, and you would typically find these brands only in specialty stores."

"How do you find these brands?" Mike asked.

"Well, sometimes they find you. A housewife-mother came walking in off the street, unannounced, with a big beach bag, and she said 'I want you to buy my son's polo shirts.' She was filled with enthusiasm, and the shirt had this little, uh, fish on it. I said 'We already have a polo shirt from Vineyard Vines, a national brand. Theirs has a whale.' She said 'Just try it.' So, we did…and it just exploded. That was Southern Tide from Greenville, just twenty-five miles away, and Vineyard Vines just became, pffft, in the past."

"And finding the next one?" Scott prodded.

"We just found the next one, it's called Southern Catch, and was suggested by one of our high-school-age employees. The owner is this young and inspired entrepreneur from Youngsville, North Carolina. Here, let me show you." Harry walked over to a display table, returning with a T-shirt. "OK, Yankees," Harry taunted as he showed us the face on the front of the shirt, "you know who that is, don't you?"

"That's, uhhh, I have no idea," Scott admitted.

"It's Robert E. Lee!" Harry pronounced. "The general's image on T-shirts has an incredible sell through."

Paul looked over Harry's shoulder at the display table, hoping a James K. Polk T-shirt might be available, but no luck.

Harry's marketing strategies revolve around communicating the stories of his regional brands. His customers face the seemingly ridiculous choice between a polo shirt with a fish or an otherwise identical polo shirt with a whale. But, of course, it's really not about the customer's favorite sea creature. Instead, the driving factor is whether the consumer identifies with— and, given that this is clothing, wants others to see that the consumer identifies with—*the story of the fish*, as communicated by the brand image that Harry constructs.

Brand image can be important any time the product says something to others about who the user of the product is. Clothing is one obvious example; you likely have a specific image in mind of what kind of person wears Gucci versus Wrangler. Beer companies do this as well: You can join the Most Interesting Man in the World by drinking Dos Equis, or you can hang out with the young and funny crowd with a Bud Light. Even a consumer electronics company can get in on the game (as Apple did) if it can somehow build hipness and cachet around its offerings. The fact that a good is consumed in public—worn on your chest, ordered in a bar, or pulled out of your pocket (as an iPhone)—is a good clue that it may be possible to build a compelling brand image.

Building such an image often requires storytelling and subtle themes and, as a result, this type of advertising is often a good fit for television. Harry chooses this medium on occasion as well, telling us "I advertise on local cable, ESPN, Fox News, Bill O'Reilly." His commercials, which we caught on YouTube, show good-looking young men wearing his regional brands and also emphasize the distinctive features of a Southern lifestyle. You wouldn't use these ads to try to sell a polo shirt to a Connecticut Yankee, and that's the whole point. Without the brand image, it's just a shirt with a fish on it; but with the brand image, it's a public symbol of regional uniqueness and Southern pride of place.

Hickory, North Carolina
CLATER KAYE THEATREWORKS

The Challenge of Marketing a "Credence Good"

In all our time on the road, we saw few branding challenges as difficult as that faced by Clater Kaye Theatreworks, which we visited back where this chapter started, in Hickory, North Carolina. Robert Clater and Lesia Kaye, an energetic and funny mixed-race married couple with a background in professional theater, met us at the door of their one-story brick facility southwest of town. We shook hands and entered the lobby, which was festooned with photographs of their young students engaged in performances of all sorts.

Lesia, fair-skinned with brown, shoulder-length hair, explained that the business is a one-stop-shop for K–12 students interested in the performing arts. "Across the country, you don't find a school like ours that offers a full set of performing arts training," she said. "You'll find a dance class, you'll find a little community theater, you'll find voice, but you don't find anything that takes a conservatory approach—like what Juilliard does at a college level. Nobody does that at a younger level."

Robert, a rotund African American with glasses, a neatly trimmed beard, and suspenders over his Clater Kaye polo, jumped in. "The bulk of what we do in this business is based on the mistakes we made during our careers. If we'd have known this, we'd have done that. We feel confident we can knock off ten years of trial and error for the young performer."

"What's on the list of mistakes you made?" Scott asked.

Lesia, who grew up in Hickory dreaming of performing on Broadway, explained. "When I started in the industry, I was always told it's all about the craft. Craft is important, don't get me wrong, but while I was busy in New York learning my lines, I wasn't busy getting to know anybody or keeping in touch with anybody after it was over."

"We have a friend, a Northwestern grad," Robert added, dropping a name and nodding at Mike. "He says this is show business, not show show or show friend."

"When they're younger, we're teaching them the craft,"

Lesia continued. "But as they get older we teach them how to network, how to present themselves, how to stay in touch without being obnoxious."

"And what the cast party's actually for—" Robert said. "It's to get the next job!"

"How did you get people in this area interested in sending their children here?" Mike offered.

"That was hard!" Lesia exclaimed quickly as everyone laughed.

"When we first started five years ago," Robert said, "there was quite a bit of community education in terms of thinking beyond the small town. It's a slow process, and it's a process we're still going through."

"When I was first getting the loan for the building," Lesia added, "the bank kept asking all these funny questions. 'Why does your application have all these people from New York listed as references?' Michael Bennett. Tommy Tune. All the names of the people we worked with. The only thing the bank was interested in was my business background. And then we started talking to parents, but they didn't know that *we really do this*—that I'm an SDC director, that Robert performed on Broadway, the fact that we directed at the Kennedy Center."

The difficulty that Robert and Lesia faced when starting out was one of establishing credibility. To sell the idea that they could help young performers avoid mistakes on their way to the Broadway stage, they had to sell their own status as experts. Presenting their credentials, however—names of show business people and the acronyms of professional organizations—just didn't mean much to a local market that was largely uneducated in the finer points of professional theater. Interestingly, the bankers seemed to know that the local parents wouldn't respond to Robert and Lesia's credentials, at least not right away, and therefore concluded that the credentials were largely irrelevant to whether the business could succeed.

The service provided by Clater Kaye is what economists call a credence good. Recall that a search good is one for which consumers can assess quality before purchase, and an experience good is one for which consumers can assess quality, but only after the good has been purchased and consumed. A credence good is one for which the consumer never completely learns about the quality of the good they have purchased or, at least, doesn't learn about quality for a very long time. For some examples, consider markets for retirement planning, basement waterproofing, or higher education. A financial planner might tell a young couple that stocks are a better choice than bonds as a retirement investment, but the couple won't know whether they've paid for good advice until they are in their sixties. A basement waterproofer could advertise that their service will keep you dry even during a one-hundred-year-flood, but it may take a while for that claim to be tested. And higher ed—well, how is a layperson to know whether the school is really teaching the very latest developments in particle physics?

At Clater Kaye, a parent is buying the expertise of Robert and Lesia, but this, of course, is a difficult thing for non-experts to assess. If Robert offers tips in class on how to navigate a Broadway cast party, how is a parent who's never been in theater to know whether the student received good advice or not? The parent sent the child to class and the student learned the lesson that was offered, but the parent is left in the dark about whether that lesson will actually be valuable for the student.

In markets for credence goods, the normal mechanism of price competition tends not to work very well. This is because customers will often use price to make an inference about the hard-to-assess quality of the good being provided. Imagine, for example, the reaction of prospective college students to a new college that announces it is offering the same quality educational experience as Stanford, but at half the price. Buying a search good like fresh produce at a discount doesn't expose you to the possibility that the vendor will skimp on quality since quality can be assessed directly. Savvy buyers will, however, always wonder how a credence good discount is being financed. Is the new college keeping the price down by skimping on hard-to-observe quality?

Credence goods present perhaps the most difficult branding challenges. As with experience goods, consumers have a hard time assessing quality prior to purchase, and this means that a strong brand can substitute for direct consumer information about the product. For experience goods, however, it's at least clear where the reputation comes from. Blind Squirrel's brand derives from the impressions of Hollywood special-effects producers and the ratings given by game reviewers, and this means Mike and Jeremy have some good starting places when they think about how to manage their brand. For credence goods, it's much harder to say what reputation is rooted in. After all, if customers cannot assess quality even after the purchase, then how exactly are reputations formed?

Because of the limited information available, brands for credence goods typically take quite some time to develop. This explains why financial institutions or elite universities manage their brands through constant reference to tradition, stability, and a long history of success. Such brands can be particularly sensitive to small pieces of information: say, one or two great success stories, or, conversely, one or two cases in which the company failed to deliver on its promises.

Robert and Lesia, realizing the near impossibility of building their brand overnight, took a patient, go-slow approach. "At the beginning, we had all the kids the other studios didn't want... Too loud for chorus or too over the top for the local community theaters," Lesia said.

"It was just like the kids in *Glee*," Robert added, laughing.

"They say you're too loud? I say you sound like Ethel Merman. You're a belter!" Lesia said as we all laughed. "We worked with them for two years, and then we self-funded a production of *Les Mis*. To help, we brought out a friend of ours who had been in the national touring company..."

"The Northwestern guy," Robert said, nodding at Mike again.

"And people couldn't believe these were *those kids*," Lesia finished, smiling.

"From there we've grown, and now we're getting kids younger and we're better able to prepare them. One of my little fellows, he's eleven. Amazing musician, and we had him singing and taking movement classes when he was young. What happens? *Billy Elliot* comes up; he's the right size, the right height, he has all the skills and he already has a callback for Broadway."

A local student with a Broadway role will build credibility in a way that a simple listing of Robert and Lesia's career accomplishments will not. But it's taken five years of very hard work for the couple to build to this level.

We thanked Robert and Lesia for the visit, regretting that

we couldn't stick around to see the kids perform. "They seemed awfully impressed that you were at Northwestern," Paul said to Mike as we drove away.

"We should have dropped the name of a Northwestern economist, just to fight back," Scott said. "Your business reminds me of the theories of Niko Matouschek... he's at Northwestern, you know."

"I was not impressed," Mike said. "Any conversation about famous Northwestern alumni in New York has to begin with Yankee manager Joe Girardi. Directing on Broadway is nothing compared to managing a diva like A-Rod."

Mazzeo's Law

Managing Your Brand: What It Depends On

- **Experience Goods:** These are products for which the customer has a difficult time assessing the quality of the product until he or she has consumed it. A primary driver of consumer choice is reputation, based on your past experience with the company or recommendations from other customers or from third-party raters, and companies like Blind Squirrel Digital manage their brand largely by managing word-of-mouth.

- **Search Goods:** These are products for which consumers can assess product quality, but only by engaging in costly search. Preston McKee reports that most pre-need customers visit only one funeral home before buying, and he therefore advertises to build brand awareness of Morris-Baker in the minds of potential customers.

- **Goods That Are Occasional or Aspirational Purchases:** For some goods, businesses need to motivate consumers to shop, and thus brand can be a persuasive message intended to generate interest. At Collins Diamonds, advertising consists of an emotional appeal to induce purchasers of luxury goods to consider a gift of jewelry.

- **Goods That Are Publicly Consumed:** For some products, brand is an image that describes what kind of person uses the product; this is particularly likely to be true when the good is consumed in public. Prices' Store for Men offers regional brands and advertises to reinforce the idea that wearing these brands is a sign of Southern pride.

- **Credence Goods:** These are products for which the consumer has a hard time assessing quality even after he or she has consumed the good. Brands for credence goods are typically built around themes of credibility and trustworthiness, and it can be difficult for new entrants like Clater Kaye Theatreworks to credibly communicate their value proposition immediately.

CHAPTER 6

Negotiating Effectively

It was a Monday morning, the first day on the road, and we were catching up.

"I haven't seen you since Snowbird," Scott said to Paul.

"Yeah, I guess that's right," Paul replied. "Amazing powder this year, huh? Remember those runs on the Cirque next to the tram?"

"Dude, that was epic," Scott said, his ski-bum vocabulary belying his middle-aged frame. "The papers were even more boring than usual, though."

Paul and Scott co-organize an economics conference each year at a ski resort not far from Scott's home in Salt Lake City. Professors present the latest research early in the morning (before the lifts open) and again in the afternoon (after they close). In between, scholars turn skiers, and attention shifts from the slope of a demand curve to, well, the slopes.

"I've been meaning to tell you guys," Mike said. "I can't do a Roadside MBA trip on those February dates we had discussed. I have to teach in Miami that week."

"Well, early January is out for me," Paul said, about to one-up Mike. "I'm going to Singapore and Thailand with our MBA students. We have some interesting meetings in Bangkok and then we spend a few days learning about ecotourism on the beaches of Phuket."

As this conversation shows, there are some good perks to being a business professor. Recently, one or more of us has traveled to Bergen on the Norwegian fjords, London, South Africa, Amsterdam, and other interesting places, all in the name of "work" (and all financed by a university or a conference organizer). It can be a pretty charmed life.

So when we arrived at our destination that morning, we could not help but wonder how we had ended up in a field of crap.

And while you'd think a field of crap would be the last thing that anyone could possibly want, we were about to learn that this particular field was the subject of some pretty intense bargaining. Negotiating well—getting the most from these bargaining situations—is a key determinant of success for many owners of small businesses. It does you no good to create value for customers only to see that value captured by suppliers or partners instead. As Mazzeo's Law suggests, the right negotiation strategies can very much depend on the particulars of the interaction.

Missoula, Montana
EKO COMPOST

Know the Other Side's Next Best Option

With its big university, natural-foods stores, and a #11 ranking on estately.com's list of best hippie towns, Missoula has a laid-back, environmentally friendly vibe. And this may explain how we ended up speaking with the ultimate in recycling-based businesses: Eko Compost.

Pulling into a dirt parking lot, we stepped out to bright early-morning sunshine. A fifty-something man, sporting an unbuttoned Hawaiian shirt, a scruffy gray beard, and long hair covered by a bandana, soon wandered over and asked about Scott's car (and, of course, the bike on top). Paul, a Deadhead since his college days in Vermont, was tempted to compare notes, but then noticed the man's T-shirt, which honored a Jimmy Buffet tribute band. The powerful aroma in the area certainly meant this was not a paradise in which to eat a cheeseburger.

We bantered with the friendly stranger for a few minutes, then began looking over his shoulder to spot the plant manager. Just then he said "I'm Phil Oakenshield, the plant manager. You must be the guys writing the book." Phil, a Vietnam veteran, has been working at the compost plant for twenty years and, when we visited, had been running the place for about a year.

The business, Phil explained as we began a tour of the facility, is composting. Now you can dress up the terminology all you like. You can say that the primary input into compost is "biosolids," and maybe that makes it sound ecological or scientific. But the fact of the matter is that we were standing in a field of crap (human crap, in fact), and this was a multiple-sense experience. It looked like crap, it felt like crap under our feet, and it *really* smelled like crap.

The biosolids, which were obtained from the municipal water treatment plant next door, were spread on an open field for acres, with several large Caterpillar earthmovers combining them with wood and other recycled organic material. Eko Compost creates piles of the mixed material and monitors temperature and moisture carefully. As a pile "cooks," bacteria break the biosolids down into carbon dioxide, water, and humus, which is a stable organic matter that makes a delightful planting soil.

The end user is a gardener planting a tree, shrub, or perennial, and this means Eko Compost's target customer is a garden center. Phil described his recent sales and marketing efforts. "Lowe's doesn't have a straight compost right now," he said. "We're trying to start small with them. Unlike Home Depot, the Lowe's districts have a little bit of latitude to try to get local products. We're working on getting distribution through their Montana district, which would be their five stores in Montana and maybe five in Idaho."

As the tour ended, we also noticed a very large conveyor belt—two or three stories high and a couple hundred feet long—positioned to dump material from the treatment plant next door onto EKO Compost's property. The City of Missoula, Phil told us when we reached his cluttered office, built the wastewater treatment facility in 1962. In 1977, EKO Compost opened up next door after negotiating an agreement to take waste from the treatment plant. The plant/compost facility combination has subsequently been copied many other places, allowing EKO Compost to be the self-proclaimed "company that started it all."

"What's your arrangement with the treatment plant?" Paul asked.

"They sell us their biosolids," Phil replied.

"You have to *buy* the biosolids?" said Scott, shocked, perhaps, that anyone would pay for such a thing.

Phil clarified: "No, no. They pay us to take it." Eko Compost is in the unusual position of earning revenue from both downstream—customers paying for their compost—and upstream, in this case the treatment plant paying them to take the biosolid input.

"What determines the price they pay?" Mike asked.

Phil proceeded to point out the advantageous position EKO Compost is in when it comes time to negotiate with the plant. "We kind of have them over a hard spot because I could say to them, 'Well, you can take it up to the BFI landfill and pay twice the amount. Or you can pay us.'"

Paul, catching on more quickly than usual, added, "I think that, once you've got the conveyor belt in, you've got them where you want them."

Phil agreed, "Yeah, because we can turn their conveyor belt off and start doing biodiesel."

This discussion points out two crucial factors that shape every negotiation: the next-best options of the parties. Negotiation is deal making, and any deal has to make the parties to that deal better off than they would be elsewhere. In this case, the next-best option for the city is to truck their biosolids to a BFI landfill. The next-best option for Eko Compost is to use their employees and facility to produce biodiesel. Any deal struck between the two has to leave both parties at least as well off as if they had chosen these alternatives instead.

Importantly, the next-best options determine what you're negotiating over—the difference between the lowest price Eko Compost would be willing to accept (enough to make composting more attractive than biodiesel) and the highest price the city would be willing to pay (if the price were above that, they'd truck the biosolids to BFI instead of using the conveyor belt). Any price within this range makes both sides happy to work together rather than pursuing their next-best option. The parties can split the difference and *both be made better off*.

Understanding the other side's next-best option is essential to negotiating well because changes in the other side's next-best option create a new range of acceptable agreements. To see why, suppose BFI raises their prices, making the city's next-best option more expensive than it was previously. The range has increased because there's more at stake for the city in the negotiation—they would be willing to pay Eko Compost more to avoid the BFI option. Eko Compost can use this change in the value of the city's next-best option to push for a higher price. The time to push for a better deal is precisely when the other side's next-best option has gotten worse or when yours has gotten better.

Phil described how this plays out with Eko Compost. "They need us more than we need them, and they keep telling us that. They keep asking us, 'You guys aren't thinking of selling or moving out?' Every time they say that, it's click, click the price up.

"Meanwhile," he continued, "we're telling them things like, 'We really don't need your biosolids. We don't really need to stay in composting here because we are into biodiesel.'"

To get the most out of the negotiation, Phil wants to make sure the city remembers that its next-best option is very expensive while also conveying that EKO Compost can do well elsewhere. Paul lamely suggested that if the negotiations went badly, Phil should simply yell, "I'm not going to take your crap anymore!" Phil chuckled politely, but we got the sense he might have heard that one before.

Jefferson City, Missouri
WREN SOLUTIONS

Improve Your Outside Options;
Reduce Your Partner's

Andy Wren, CEO of Wren Solutions, was kind enough to provide a thorough explanation of his company's products and operations, as well as an interesting tour of his company's Jefferson City, Missouri, facility. And some day we hope to meet him.

While Andy was enthusiastic about talking with us when we contacted him, he explained there was one important caveat. Wren's corporate headquarters are in Jefferson City, but Andy and several parts of the operation are based in Atlanta. So our meeting consisted of the three of us sitting in a conference room in Missouri talking at a speakerphone with Andy, who sat two states away in Georgia.

"This is unusual," Scott said as we waited alone in a beige conference room with a wood table large enough to seat the presidential cabinet.

"It's perfect," Mike quipped. "Now I can silently mock you when you ask a stupid question."

When he joined our conversation, Andy explained the odd geography of the situation. "I grew up in Jeff City, went to Auburn, and majored in sports marketing. With the Olympics coming here in 1996, this seemed like the place to be. Then I decided to go to work for Dad, but there's no baseball team in Jefferson City. I love Jeff City, but when I was twenty-three years old it didn't seem as attractive as Atlanta from a quality-of-life perspective."

Wren Solution's main business is security systems, manufacturing housings and mounts for cameras, and developing solutions for monitoring. Wren originally focused on retail customers but has now expanded to other markets, particularly school systems.

Walmart, Wren's biggest customer, uses their systems to watch customers from cameras mounted in the ceiling. "To frame up our industry, imagine a pyramid with three horizontal layers," Andy explained. "The bottom of the pyramid is what we call system components. It's very hardware-centric, it's the plastic housings, the cameras, the monitors, and the recording platforms. That was our whole industry up through the 1990s. That segment of the market is not the bottom of the pyramid and it is essentially a commodity business.

"As technology advanced, things shifted to digital video, so software started to make an entree into the business. We've now got 'point' solutions, where we have software driving some of those cameras and recording devices. That layer is where we are as an industry right now. The top is more of a pure software play, trying to integrate all those systems. That's where we have positioned our business moving forward."

Further discussion with Andy revealed that negotiating with customers, as well as setting the company's strategy in anticipation of those negotiations, is essential to the success of Wren Solutions. Their experiences highlight the value of thinking strategically about how to improve your own next-best option and how to find partners whose next-best options are not so strong.

Paul got right to the heart of the issue. "Walmart has a reputation of being very hard on their suppliers. Are there downsides to having so much of your business with them?" Mike did not silently mock this, so it must have been a decent question.

Andy explained that Wren works very hard to avoid being "just another supplier" to Walmart. "It's less about the products sometimes and more about helping them address issues. As a tangible example, we now do system design work for Walmart. They were having some bottlenecks and we have a CAD [computer-aided design] group, so they give us a store layout and we do the heavy lifting on designing the video surveillance system."

"So they have a general design, but you help them figure out exactly what wire needs to go where?" Scott asked.

"Yes, we generate the bill of materials for them," Andy replied, probably nodding, but we couldn't really tell. "That's not our core business, but it's finding ways to solve problems for our key customers."

Wren has put itself in a strong negotiating position by find-

ing ways to limit the attractiveness of Walmart's next-best option. In order to walk away from a negotiation with Wren,
Walmart would have to find a replacement for both Wren's
hardware and Wren's system design work. By bundling commoditized hardware with harder-to-replace expertise, Wren reduces the relative value of Walmart's next-best option and
makes it easier for Wren to capture value.

Mike asked, "Don't you worry about making a lot of investments in terms of spending time on design for just one
customer?"

Andy's response made clear that he thinks quite hard about
his own next-best option, as well as Walmart's. "That could be
a concern, but anything we do, we look at the greater market.
We don't want to just build custom solutions, so we are out
talking to other customers about that same type of solution to
make sure the thing is saleable elsewhere." While Wren works
closely with Walmart, it always has an eye on alternatives, including the education market.

The negotiating challenges are different for Wren in the
education sector, and Andy described the company's process
for assessing various market segments. "We didn't go after the
biggest school districts because things there are price driven.
With the big districts, it's the lowest bid. We didn't go after the
smallest because we don't think there's enough return for us.
But the mid-sized world was very underserved. Much of the
competition was local mom-and-pop outfits, and in many cases
they weren't as current with technology. We'd rather go after
the smaller sale and come in with more technical savvy, allowing us to build significant credibility by referencing our big
retail customers like Walmart."

In education, Wren has targeted specifically those customers with weaker next-best options. Other bidders pursue the large-district segment aggressively, and procurement rules mean that Wren has little opportunity to improve its bargaining position by bundling service and expertise with its products. Options available to mid-sized districts are more limited, however, and Wren can offer a product that greatly improves on the next-best options of those customers.

Slidell, Louisiana
GAYLORD CHEMICAL

Anticipate to Avoid Exploitation

Slidell, Louisiana, is an upscale suburb of New Orleans, about thirty miles northeast of Bourbon Street and across Lake Pontchartrain. We visited in early February, and the mood in town was festive: Both Mardi Gras and the Super Bowl were imminent. The Comfort Inn lobby was decorated with masks, and the young front desk clerk had donned, halfheartedly, a couple of strands of beads. Locating a lakeside restaurant, we shared the dining room with a large group of New Jersey football fans and struggled to communicate with each other as the Garden-Staters loudly debated whether to take the Ravens and the points.

The next day, we skipped the festivities and headed to the office of Gaylord Chemical, where we met with Paul Dennis, the president and CEO. Bespectacled, middle-aged, and wearing a simple dress shirt and blue sweater, Paul D. looked like he would be more at home at, well, a convention of chemical executives (or economists) than at the Mardi Gras celebrations that were about to overtake him. Gaylord's headquarters, which we'd easily have mistaken for a doctor's office, houses fewer than ten people, with most of Gaylord's thirty or so employees located at a plant in Alabama, a few hours' drive away.

Gaylord is a leading producer of a chemical called DMSO (dimethyl sulfoxide), a solvent that has a variety of applications from industrial (paint and photoresist stripping) to pharmaceutical (drug delivery), and began as part of the paper company Crown Zellerbach. "They were keen to find commercial value for other chemicals that were in the black liquor," Paul D. explained. "Black liquor is a stream that is created in a paper mill during the extraction of the pulp. It isn't useful for paper except for its energy value, but it can be rich in all kinds of chemicals." To use this by-product, Crown Zellerbach developed a process for extracting methyl groups from the black liquor. The methyl groups can then be used, in combination with sulfur, to make DMSO.

After a series of spin-offs and corporate transactions, Paul D. and his colleagues bought the business, but they were required as part of their purchase to relocate the company's plant. Because Gaylord's process combines methyl groups (from a paper mill) with sulfur (which is a by-product of oil refining), it made sense to partner either with a paper mill or an oil refinery, and then to build a new plant adjacent to an important supplier.

"We talked with many refineries across the country, including one in Alabama," Paul D. recalled. "They were doing an expansion and needed an additional outlet for their sulfur gas. It was a good deal for both parties because, given our substantial customer base, the demand for the sulfur gas would be immediate and substantial. Also, the refinery's alternative was to make additional elemental sulfur, which is corrosive—it can destroy expensive manufacturing equipment. Our process is not corrosive, and we pay for the expenses incurred in producing and marketing the final product."

To bring the manufacturing partnership to fruition, both parties were required to make substantial investments in infrastructure. Because sulfur gas cannot be easily transported, these investments tie Gaylord to the refinery physically—their partnership is even tighter than the Eko Compost relationship with the wastewater treatment plant.

"That is a big commitment," Scott commented, understanding the potential consequences. "How does the partnership work?"

Paul D. started out by noting the partnership's origins, "Before we relocated our DMSO plant, we agreed to a long-term arrangement that divides the production responsibilities between the refinery and Gaylord. We also negotiated a longterm agreement to use land on their site. If either party decides the arrangement no longer works, the party is required to give many years' notice."

Negotiating a good agreement *before* building their plant was critical because making this investment changes Gaylord's next-best option and hurts their bargaining position. Prior to construction, Gaylord's next-best option to a deal with the Alabama refinery was pretty good; there are other refineries looking to get rid of sulfur gas, and Gaylord could have struck a reasonable agreement with one of them. Once the plant is built, however, Gaylord cannot walk away from the refinery without forfeiting the large sum it has invested in this new facility. Gaylord's next-best option becomes very poor indeed.

And as we noted above in discussing Eko Compost, when the other side's next-best option gets worse, it's exactly the time to push for a better deal. In the absence of an up-front arrangement, the refinery could exploit Gaylord's weakened bargaining position in a number of ways. For example, the refinery could threaten to cut the flow of inputs unless Gaylord agreed to pay a higher price to the refinery. Gaylord might have no choice but to acquiesce simply because the alternative would involve shuttering a hugely expensive DMSO plant. This issue cuts both ways, of course; Gaylord could also try to extract concessions by refusing to take the refiner's sulfur. This would force the refiner into an expensive alternative for getting rid of the stuff. Economists refer to this as the "holdup problem"—like a masked gunman, one party could simply "rob" the other once the deal is made, the plant is built, and the next-best options have changed.

A long-term contract, like the one between Gaylord and the refinery, is a good start toward a solution to this problem. It can go a long way toward ensuring that the relationship fits the needs of both parties and permits both sides to invest in the partnership.

To work perfectly, however, such a contract would need to specify all the possible ways in which the refinery and Gaylord could hold each other up, and then include language forbidding those actions. We wondered whether the initial long-term agreement solved all potential issues between Gaylord and the refinery.

"What do you do if conflicts come up?" Mike asked.

"Sometimes there are gray areas where it's unclear who is responsible," Paul D. replied. "We have a steering team between the two companies that deals with any unforeseen issues. We are very transparent with them, and we expect them to be very transparent with us."

This statement illustrates that there are always limits to contracts, and no written agreement can anticipate every issue that might arise. Managing the relationship with the refinery is therefore an important part of Paul D.'s job. "Their objective is to get rid of waste material. To us, it's lifeblood. However, they do a good job of addressing our issues."

Dothan, Alabama
PANHANDLE CONVERTER RECYCLING

Better Information Leads to Better Deals

While we passed on extracurricular activities in the New Orleans area, we couldn't resist the local color during our time in Dothan, Alabama. Dothan, we learned prior to our visit, proudly proclaims itself the "Peanut Capital of the World." This is an unofficial distinction—at least six cities in the United States lay claim to the title—but Dothan is, at worst, the Peanut Capital of Alabama. One quarter of the US peanut crop is harvested within seventy-five miles of Dothan, and the fairgrounds south of town hosts the National Peanut Festival for two weeks each fall. Our visit, unfortunately, did not coincide with the Peanut Festival, but we did make a point of hitting the other peanut-related attraction in Dothan.

"It says there's a gold Peanut Monument right next to the visitors' center," Mike said from the backseat as we drove across town on our lunch break.

Arriving, we parked and exited the rental car, and then came upon it: a not-quite-waist-high bronze-ish replica of the honorable legume.

"This is it?" Mike whined. "It's hardly bigger than an actual peanut."

"It looked so big in the pictures," Paul agreed, disappointed. "I was imagining something more like the Washington Monument."

"Well, this would be the George Washington Carver Monument, right?" Scott said.

"Well, no," Mike corrected. "I read there's an actual monument to him down on the fairgrounds."

"Well, give Dothan credit for trying," Paul said. "Sacramento claims to be the almond capital, but I'm not aware of any statuary."

Shrugging off our disappointment, we snapped a few photos and headed across town to meet with Lyle Peluso Jr. Lyle is the chief operating officer of a small (less than fifty employees) but very productive ($78 million revenue) company called Panhandle Converter Recycling. Lyle looked somewhat like Mike on a teaching day—nice suit and tie, almost no hair on top, and about a day's worth of stubble that indicated either fashion sense or laziness. He originally joined Panhandle through a contact from his church.

"Joe Donovan [Panhandle's CEO and founder] and I went on a mission trip together to Africa," Lyle said. "My dad is his pastor. I was going to speak on basic leadership stuff, while he

was going to help build the roof on a school. We rode to Atlanta together and started talking about his business, as we had
at various times before. I was studying business intelligence
from an IT perspective at the time—relational databases and
the like. So we started having running conversations—'You
should do this, you should do that.' Then he hired me to do
the IT and let me implement all these ideas."

The enthusiasm that won Lyle the job still carries over.
His animated tour of Panhandle's noisy recycling facility
included a steady stream of surprises and plenty of interesting economics. The four of us, all wearing suits,
were badly out of place in the large, dusty warehouse.
On the left were several bays where junk dealers could
bring in catalytic converters by the truckload. Large piles
of converters—rectangular or cylindrical metal housings at-
tached to exhaust-pipe stubs on either end—sat in the center
of the warehouse. To the right, a couple of burly employees
holding clipboards were processing converters, sorting them
into a series of large wire bins a couple feet deep, wide,
and across. Catalytic converters, Lyle explained, are an essential part of every automobile's emissions control system
and convert toxic by-products of gasoline combustion into
less harmful substances.

Panhandle's main business is breaking these used catalytic
converters apart and recycling the innards. In particular, the
converters contain small amounts of three precious metals:
palladium, platinum, and rhodium. "We are in the commodities business," Lyle said. "Or, as I call it, urban mining. It's
a lot cheaper for everyone. It's a lot safer for everyone. It's
cleaner. We're not in South Africa, fracking, or anything like

that. The metals are already out there. They just need to be pulled back in."

Panhandle recovers the precious metals with a fifteen-foot-high machine that breaks open the metal housing, smashes the ceramic inside of the converter, and collects the remains. The result is a gray-white powdery dust that, stored in clear plastic bags, looks a bit like a prop from an episode of *Miami Vice*. The output is valuable, but there is a well-developed market for these commodities, so there is not much scope for negotiation on the selling price. Panhandle sells the output to large manufacturers—most of the recycled material ends up in the catalytic converters of newly manufactured cars—and earns revenue based on the current market prices of the metals.

"Where does the IT and business intelligence come in?" Paul asked, impressed by the surroundings, but as yet unclear on the value proposition.

Lyle explained that it is hard to tell what metals, and how much, are present in any given converter that a junk dealer might bring in. "Every manufacturer uses a different methodology for putting the precious metals in there, and they all use different amounts. It depends on what the market prices were when they were made. If platinum is through the roof and palladium is low, it's cheaper to double the amount of palladium you put into it. Year, make, model, emissions standards—all these things factor in." Without some sense for what metals are in what converters, any negotiation between Panhandle and a junk dealer over a load of converters is based largely on guesswork. Sometimes Panhandle would overpay and lose money, while other times they would underpay and earn a windfall.

"Yeah, we're trying to solve that a little bit," Lyle said.

"When the business started, Joe realized some catalytic converters had something the other ones didn't. He was sending things off to the refiner so he could figure out what metals were in certain model types. He started saving all this information about what was in different converters. For months before I ever officially came on board, we would dialogue often about how to better organize his historical data on spreadsheets and brainstorm about how to use this information strategically."

While the market for precious metals—Lyle's output—is commoditized, the market for used converters—his input—is not. As a result, negotiating with the junk dealers to buy at the right price is a key to success for Panhandle. "We have a price sheet that's based on thousands and thousands of catalytic converters that are put into many categories," Lyle told us. "There's an algorithm that takes the price of platinum, palladium, and rhodium and then it tells us what we should pay for each category today."

This information puts Panhandle in an excellent negotiating position with the suppliers of its key input. When a junk dealer brings a load of converters to the dock, Panhandle offers a price based on sorting the converters into categories and applying their data-driven algorithm. This greatly reduces the sometimes-you-win, sometimes-you-lose guesswork and gives Panhandle great confidence to walk away from deals that will be losers.

Panhandle is taking this information advantage even one step further. Recognizing that the uncertainty about what metals are in the converters generates inefficiencies in their dealings with junk dealers, they are investing in laboratory equipment that will allow them to pay dealers based on *exactly* what is inside their catalytic converters. "What we want to do is obliterate categories altogether. We want the junkyard owners to send us the converters, let us run them through the machinery (it only takes an hour for a ton), then we take a sample over to the lab, and, a couple of hours later, we will tell you exactly how much platinum, rhodium, and palladium you have and we'll broker it directly. We'll just take a percentage. We want to change the whole way they do it."

Enid, Oklahoma
PT COUPLING

Be Prepared to Walk Away and Do It Yourself

If you're a *New York Times* crossword puzzle fan as Paul is, then you'd derive a certain sense of satisfaction from pulling into "US city named for a Tennyson character" or "the seat of Garfield County" or, early in the week, a four-letter word for an Oklahoma city. But when we arrived in Enid, Oklahoma, on a Wednesday evening in January, it was so dark and so cold that we were using a different set of four-letter words when we exited the car. The high temperature during our time in Enid was twenty Fahrenheit (-7 Celsius). The low? A bitter seven degrees Fahrenheit. Google Maps told us we were some seventy miles farther south than Paul's home in Palo Alto, but it certainly didn't feel like it.

Despite the cold, we had a productive visit the following afternoon with PT Coupling, a manufacturer located on US 64 northeast of town. There we met with Jim Parrish, the long-time company president, and his son Matt, who had recently taken the reins. Jim and Matt looked like father and son, with full heads of hair and bushy eyebrows. Matt sported a nicely pressed black dress shirt with the PT Coupling logo subtly embroidered above the pocket, while Jim wore a simple green-checked button-down. Matt deferred to his father in most of the interview, allowing him to describe the business.

"This is a business that was started by my father in 1951 as a machine shop," Jim explained. "In 1955, the patent expired on the cam and groove coupling, and we started producing that at that time."

A coupling, we learned, is a hose fitting. It's the piece of metal that would attach, for example, to one of Charlie Centhner's fire hoses and allow you to connect the hose to a hydrant or pumping truck. Couplings come in various sizes to fit various sizes of hose and are workhorses of industrial life.

"When we started," Jim continued, "we had no foundry. We were just a machine shop. We were buying our castings from local foundries and machining them here."

"What is the role of the foundry in the process of making a coupling?" Scott asked.

"In order to make a hose fitting, you have to have some kind of a shape to start with," Jim replied. "A foundry makes a sand mold and then pours molten metal into that mold to come up with a general shape, then you machine it to the precise shape. We struggled to find a foundry that would perform to our needs on quantities, delivery, and quality. For years we tried to buy stainless steel from a sand foundry with very poor results, so many parts were rejected because of casting defects."

Realizing that these other foundries were disappointing a

customer, Mike inquired "Why couldn't these other foundries get it figured out?"

"These were jobbing foundries," Jim answered, meaning the foundries served many customers and were not captive to any of them. "We were a very small company at the time, and it was difficult for us to demand the attention to get them to do what was necessary to produce to our specifications."

It is not surprising that a small machine shop like PT Coupling would have trouble getting larger foundries to make investments in improving quality. Put yourself in the shoes of such a foundry, and imagine a small customer asking you to make an investment in process improvements that will be valued only by that small customer. While it's certain that PT Coupling would have been willing to pay for the extra quality, a foundry would face two big risks. First, any investment that is useful only to PT Coupling would be subject to the hold-up problem discussed earlier. What's to stop PT Coupling from demanding a lower price once the foundry has made its investments? Second, there's little guarantee that a small customer like PT Coupling will survive long.

Given this, it's easy to see why a foundry would make exorbitant price demands in order to meet PT Coupling's specs or even refuse to negotiate in the first place. And so PT Coupling learned a fundamental lesson of negotiations. When the value of the relationship is worse than your next-best option, stop negotiating. Even though it was a small business, PT Coupling made a tough choice. "We never found a foundry that was satisfactory, so we decided to start our own."

Paul asked, "So once you became your own supplier, did performance improve?"

Jim shook his head. "We struggled for some time until we were able to get to where we needed to be."

In order to keep all parts of the business honest, PT Coupling makes sure its foundry is selling to outside customers and the machine shop is buying from outside foundries. According to Jim, "Our goal has always been to *not* be a completely captive foundry or machine shop. The quality that we produce is important, and we get better feedback if we are supplying the product to other people rather than just to ourselves."

In other words, whether dealing with internal or external partners, the value of the next-best option crucially shapes negotiated outcomes. PT Coupling's machine shop buys from the PT Coupling foundry but also maintains relationships with other vendors. This guarantees that the machine shop has a quality outside option and can walk away from deals with the PT Coupling foundry if quality standards are not met. The reverse holds true as well, so strong next-best options keep all parts of the company focused on quality.

And so, having learned the limits of negotiation and when it may make sense to go it alone, we left Enid behind and headed to Oklahoma City for our flights home. As we drove, we realized that all of us—even Mike, who was heading home to Chicago—would soon be in a much warmer place.

"Next road trip, let's think about the weather before we decide where we are going to go," suggested Scott.

We all heartily agreed—no negotiations were necessary.

Mazzeo's Law

Negotiating Effectively: What It Depends On

- **Next-Best Options:** A key determinant of outcomes in any negotiation is each party's next-best option relative to working together. Eko Compost could choose to make biodiesel, and the adjacent wastewater plant could truck its biosolids to the landfill; any deal has to be preferable for both parties.

- **Ability to Influence Next-Best Options:** Wren provides solutions instead of just products so that Walmart's next-best option is less attractive. But when a big school district solicits bids from a large number of potential suppliers, Wren avoids the deal because it doesn't want to be one of several alternatives.

- **Investments and Hold-Up:** Gaylord Chemical tied its fortunes to those of its partner by making a large fixed investment in a co-located plant. Gaylord's next-best option gets dramatically worse once this investment is made, so Gaylord negotiated an agreement up front, while it still had better options available.

- **Information:** Having more information puts you in a powerful negotiating position. By knowing more about what it is buying, Panhandle Converters ensures that it always gets a good deal.

- **Whether You Can Go It Alone:** When the value of the relationship is worse than your next-best option, stop negotiating. Unable to find a foundry to provide quality parts, PT Coupling decided to start its own foundry and ensures quality by making sure its upstream and downstream divisions have the strong next-best option of working with outside suppliers and customers.

CHAPTER 7

Hiring

It's hard to fully appreciate the word "swelter" unless you've been in Missouri during a summer heat wave. This we learned in Saint Joseph, located on the western border of the state about fifty miles north of Kansas City, during a mid-August visit. A cheery desk clerk checked us in at the Stoney Creek Inn, which was packed with fans in town to watch the NFL's Kansas City Chiefs train at nearby Missouri Western State University. The Stoney Creek Inn takes its Wild West theme very seriously, with a massive stone fireplace, rustic wooden staircase railings, picture frames that look like rifles, and a buffalo mural by the indoor pool. The proprietors also take their air-conditioning seriously, which was a wonderful relief after our rental-car AC struggled to get the interior temperature under eighty on the drive from Jefferson City. We pulled the wool blankets up high and slept great.

It was already in the mid-eighties headed for a high of ninety-eight when we met at the front desk after breakfast in the immaculate dining room. "I like this place," said Mike, our motel aficionado. "Good breakfast, comfortable bed, great service."

"Yeah, but I wish they had more stuffed deer heads on the wall," Paul said. "Skimp on the linens if you have to, but not on taxidermy."

"That's an elk," Scott corrected.

"Paul, get some photos. I am digging the whole Pony Express vibe," Mike added.

Paul snapped a few interiors, and then we headed out to the car. As Mike and Scott loaded the trunk, Paul took one of the most memorable photographs we have from all our travels. The extreme AC of the Stoney Creek Inn had cooled the lens of his camera down to about sixty-five degrees. Then the extreme humidity of western Missouri provided ample water vapor, which quickly condensed onto the chilled lens. In the photo, you can barely make out the outline of a building—the Stoney Creek Inn backlit by a bright, smeared-out sun. About the only detail discernible through the fog is the outline of moose antlers from a statue out front. The photo screams MUGGY, and we were nearly soaked through in our suits, sport coats, and ties after about ten seconds of standing in the parking lot.

Driving away, we continued our conversation about the Stoney Creek Inn. While the decor might have been John Wayne, the service, we decided, was more along the lines of Tom Hanks: friendly, approachable, and attentive. Having acclimated to indifferent (or occasionally hostile) service at roadside motels, this came as a bit of a surprise. "I think it comes down to the hiring," Paul offered. "It doesn't matter what else you do if you've got the wrong people in place."

"Sure," Mike agreed, "but how are they doing it? Hiring is notoriously difficult."

"Call them back and see if you can get a meeting on our way out of town," Scott said. "If they've got a silver hiring bullet, we want to know."

On our many travels, we searched long and hard for hiring solutions, but, as Mazzeo's Law would suggest, there's really no silver bullet. This task is just plain hard, and even skillful, experienced managers make mistakes. We did, however, run across some useful strategies that can make a company's hiring process more effective. Understanding how and why these strategies work is the first step toward determining whether they'll work for you.

Saint Joseph, Missouri
SOUTHSIDE FAMILY FUN CENTER

Improve Your Applicant Pool by Playing Hard to Get

We took the Belt Highway south through Saint Joseph and rolled to a stop in the dusty gravel parking lot of the Southside Family Fun Center. Inside we found twenty-four lanes of bowling along with a snack bar and a lounge. Richard Shuster, a bearded man in his fifties wearing khakis and a yellow polo shirt, greeted us with a handshake and a smile.

"My wife and I bought this place in March of 2008," Richard began, his speech occupying the gray area between a Midwestern twang and a Southern drawl. "It had sat empty for maybe three years and was in bad shape. My wife and I had bowled for twenty-plus years, and there's just no entertainment in the south end. There's maybe some old dive bars, but no family-type entertainment."

Richard explained that the south side is the older, industrial part of Saint Joseph. The stockyards and the packing houses were here, and a strong industrial presence, with major manufacturers of cans and batteries, remains. Local residents are blue collar, and unemployment is a problem.

"There are two other bowling centers in town," he continued, "and we have to price to what our south end people can afford. There's just more money out on the east side of town. We charge $2.50 per game to bowl, and our competitors are over $3.00, and one's right at $4.00 per game. It's a huge difference. The other two places have better locations, and our facility is also much older, but we try to outrank them by being cleaner."

"I was just thinking that!" Mike interjected. "This is the cleanest bowling alley I've ever seen in my life."

"Exactly. My wife and I are clean freaks—she doesn't work here, but when she gets off work managing inventory at the local food bank, she comes down here and gets her rag out. That's one of the big things that our employees know to do. We've worked with them, we've trained them, they know that's the way we want things done."

"But your pricing really limits what you can do for your employees on wages, right?" Scott noted. "How do you find people who can execute the way you need?"

"Finding the right people is a huge challenge," Richard admitted. "We put an ad in the paper back when we were getting started. The job was for a floater, somebody to cover any position, and it paid minimum wage. In one day, we had a hundred and seventy-six people come through that front door to apply."

As the story of this one vacancy illustrates, finding the right person is often like finding a needle in a haystack, especially when using a "post and pray" approach. Like many employers, Richard says he needs "drive, desire, and passion" more than he needs any particular skill set, but spotting drive can be tough since it's all too easy to fake it with an enthusiastic interview or a few choice action verbs on a résumé.

Screening candidates, whether it's reviewing résumés, conducting interviews, or checking references, is costly. Time spent doing interviews is time a small business owner isn't spending on other essential activities. Hence, it's important to minimize the cost of screening when possible, and also to balance the cost of screening against the benefit of making better hires.

At Southside Family Fun Center, Richard reduced the cost of screening by playing hard to get. That is, he set up small hurdles that an applicant must overcome in order to have his or her application receive consideration. Note first that Richard required applicants to apply in person. This might well be a hassle for applicants—especially compared to an on-line job application process—but this is precisely what Richard wants. To see why, imagine two potential job applicants: one who knows that she's a good match for Richard's job and stands a good chance of getting an offer, and another who doesn't care much for bowling or cleaning and figures he's a long shot to get an offer. The first applicant is the needle in the haystack, and Richard very much wants her to apply. The second, though, is just hay, and more hay in the stack means more costly screening work to identify the good candidate from among a mass of résumés. Richard would prefer that the second simply not apply.

The key to this logic is that job seekers compare cost and benefit when making decisions about what jobs to apply for. A person who has little chance of getting an offer won't bother with the hassle of applying. If, on the other hand, that same person thinks she's a great fit for this job, then the hassle cost probably won't deter her. A small hassle cost of applying deters hay more than it does needle and means that Richard's overall pool of applicants is tilted a bit more toward better candidates.

Note, however, that Richard still got 176 applications (likely attributable in part to the high local unemployment rate). How could he work through this pile of paper efficiently? Richard described his next step: "We put right on the ad 'Bring a pen,' and the first five through the door didn't have a pen. So I just said, 'How do you expect to get a job when you don't pay attention to the rules?' People just scattered! They ran outside and were getting pens here and there. They came back in and filled out their applications. At the end of the day, there weren't but five that we were interested in talking to."

Surely Richard had pens sitting around the bowling alley back office; this is not about the pens. Instead, Richard is putting up a second hurdle. To receive serious consideration, an applicant had to read the ad carefully enough to know to bring a pen. Again, this is precisely the sort of small cost that will tilt the pool in a favorable direction. The applicants who think they are a good match for the job will be more fastidious in reading instructions than those who think they are a long shot. The play-hard-to-get strategy works by giving serious applicants the opportunity to separate themselves from the rest by incurring small costs that demonstrate their belief that they're credible candidates. By playing hard to get, Richard was able to reduce his pool to a manageable five, and it was this group that received a full résumé review, interview, and reference check.

It's often counterintuitive to managers when we encourage them to play hard to get. If I'm serious about hiring, people wonder, then why would I want to discourage applications? The answer is that it's always good to deter applications from bad matches; the last thing you want is a bigger haystack when what you need is that one elusive needle.

And while Richard's hiring problem was indeed difficult, he did catch one break: "We had a few people come in that day wearing pajamas," he said, shaking his head and laughing. None of these individuals made the second round.

Pensacola, Florida
RE VERA SERVICES

Consider Wages and Productivity When Posting Jobs

A different sort of hiring challenge is faced by Re Vera Services, a start-up in Pensacola, Florida, that provides verification services for higher educational institutions. Steve Nolen, a stocky, dark-haired graduate of the United States Naval Academy and MIT's MBA program, met us in a conference room, while his co-founder and wife, Carla, tended to their five-week-old in the back office, listening to our conversation by speakerphone.

"Our business," Steve began, "is to validate the information that admitted students listed on their applications to top MBA programs. Suppose, for example, somebody says they worked for Goldman Sachs as an associate, or they have a degree in philosophy from Princeton. We make sure that information is correct, and the only way to do that for sure is go to the source."

This piqued the interest of all of us since that's our students he's talking about!

"We'll get a list from a school of students and the information they want verified. Then it's dial and smile. We employ seventeen people, and we're calling all over the world."

"Can you give us an example of what sorts of problems you find?" Scott asked as Carla, casually dressed and with long blond hair, joined us in the conference room after the baby fell asleep, the speakerphone acting as a baby monitor.

"Different schools are looking at different things," Carla replied. "Let's say the student listed that he worked at Deutsche Bank as an analyst. We might find out he was an intern/analyst, and that might be relevant for some schools. We find a lot of degrees that aren't completed; maybe they finished all the credits, but didn't apply for graduation or pay their final bill."

"This is really interesting," Paul said, eyebrows raised. His mind was obviously wandering back to his home campus in California.

Mike knew exactly what Paul was thinking. "You want to ask about a specific student you had, don't you? Me too! I had this guy last semester.... He surely must have falsified something to get in!"

The business, which was started in 2005, grew out of a job Carla took in the MIT MBA admissions office while Steve was a student. "They were just piloting their verification program," Steve explained, "and she spent the summer building the process. Then they handed it off to a large company to do the actual verifying, and the amount of information that came back was really overwhelming."

Carla explained that this wasn't because the amount of application fraud was itself overwhelming, but rather that the verifier was flagging every single mismatch—no matter how small. "Suppose a student working at a bank applies to business school in November, and he puts $105,000 as his best guess for total pay once annual bonuses are released in December. Then the bonus comes out, and the actual annual pay is $103,000. A discrepancy like that was getting flagged, and then the admissions staff would have to put resources into figuring it out. For a large MBA class—Harvard admits maybe nine hundred students annually—the admissions team simply doesn't have the resources to follow up on seven hundred flags."

"We work with the admissions office to get a sense of what they think is material, and then we limit the flags to the issues they really ought to be taking a close look at," Steve said.

This discussion raises the following question: What's the right number of flags? Too many flags and you're overwhelming the admissions staff with trivial details. But with too few flags—meaning important mismatches aren't being caught—well, you get students like the one Mike was complaining about. In an extreme case, an unflagged application could do serious damage to the school's reputation. It would be difficult, perhaps impossible, for the client to know whether they're getting too few flags, and this means the service provided by Re Vera is a great example of a credence good. (Recall our discussion of Clater Kaye Theatreworks in chapter 5). As Carla and Steve are acutely aware, reputation and trust are especially important in markets for credence goods, and Steve summarized the issue well: "Schools have to trust that you're going to do what you need to do to conduct the verification."

Maintaining clients' trust means that Re Vera can ill afford mistakes, and this fact has important implications for hiring strategy. Steve described the job as "essentially a call-center employee; you could get somebody for minimum wage, maybe a little more." But the extreme quality imperative means Re Vera can't survive with the average call-center employee; instead, it needs a 99th-percentile call-center employee. "We overpay for our people," Steve said. "We offer an hourly rate that's twice what we should be paying."

Scott nodded but then asked. "Why do you say you 'overpay'? If you buy a Mercedes because you really value the quality, did you overpay just because you could have gotten a Camry for less?"

Steve thought for a minute. "I see what you're saying. A lot of our employees are well educated. They're stay-at-home moms with masters degrees or further. At times I think we even underpay relative to the quality of the person we get."

"I totally agree," said Carla.

The contrast between Southside Family Fun Center, which hires at minimum wage, and Re Vera, which could fill openings at minimum wage but chooses not to, brings up an important point: It pays to be strategic about where to position on the employee quality/wage scale. While too-high wages can certainly eat into an employer's profits, it's probably not the case that employers should be seeking the cheapest possible help. Why? Well, you get what you pay for, and the cheapest possible employee probably wouldn't get much done. Conversely, while productivity is good, it's probably not the case that the most productive possible employee is the one you want; highly talented people can be expensive to retain.

If the right employee isn't the cheapest but also isn't the most productive, then who is the right employee?

The optimal trade-off between quality and wages happens when the difference between productivity and wage is maximized. And this maximize-the-difference quality level is likely to be at a different place for different companies. At Re Vera, for example, minimum-wage employees would be inexpensive but would probably require heavy supervisory oversight in order to hit the company's quality standards. And the cost of this supervisory overhead might well be larger than the savings associated with hiring at this lower wage. Steve and Carla Nolen are, as a result, best off with more expensive but more capable employees. Southside Family Fun Center could probably hire more able employees by paying a dollar an hour above minimum wage. But how much would this additional ability be worth? If the job is to clean tables and a better (and more expensive) employee cleans tables 30 percent faster, will this somehow translate to higher revenues? For Richard Shuster, a faster table cleaner may not be worth the additional cost.

Enid, Oklahoma
AEROSOCK

Design Jobs to Discourage the Wrong Applicants

We saw another notable hiring strategy late one morning in Oklahoma. We had all gotten a good night's sleep at the local Ramada—nice enough, but completely lacking in taxidermy—but that didn't stop Paul and Scott from their usual Thursday grousing.

"We are having lunch where?" Paul asked.

"Country club. Chamber president invited us to their monthly buffet luncheon," Scott replied, then paused before meekly adding "I think there's an economist from the state speaking."

"Noooooooooooo!!!!" Paul and Mike jointly howled. Even other economists, it seems, think that state-government economists make boring lunchtime speakers.

"If he shows a graph of national versus state-level unemployment, I am going to slit my wrists with my butter knife," Paul exclaimed.

"I'm going to skip the buffet and order a steak off the menu just so they'll bring me a sharper knife," Mike quipped.

"Look, the Chamber here was really helpful, so you're going to go and you're going to stay awake," Scott pronounced, using his best stern-parent voice. "You especially," he added, glancing sideways at Paul, who is well known around Stanford for nodding off during academic seminars.

We parked and met Donna Lemmons, owner of Aerosock, who showed us to her brightly lit space inside the James W. Strate Business Development Center. Petite, wearing a green sweater and glasses, Donna makes quite a first impression. She's a high-energy straightshooter, clearly not the kind of manager who puts up with a lot of bull.

"My husband started this business in the mid-eighties. He worked for Texaco in Hobbs, New Mexico, and one day overheard an oil field operator say, 'I just wish we could find a windsock that would last!' He was single then and had always wanted to run a business, so he did some research and started a small side business making windsocks. He cut patterns on the weekends and hired seamstresses. His innovation was to find higher-quality fabrics, and it started out small, with oil field customers in Hobbs, but then grew to other areas: aviation, refrigeration, prisons, wastewater treatments, air medical."

"So I can understand the aviation applications...," Mike interjected.

"Prisons have tear gas," Donna interrupted. "Anytime you have the possibility of something airborne that could be pushed by the wind, you better have windsocks to see where it's going."

Not having spent much time at prisons, the three of us tried to recall whether there were windsocks on the *Shawshank Redemption* set.

"I got involved in the business twelve or thirteen years ago, when we got married," Donna continued. "At the time I had a freelance court-reporting business, so we officed that and Aerosock together." Donna described various twists and turns in life and her career—including five years as an elected judge in New Mexico—that eventually led the couple to move themselves and Aerosock to Enid to be closer to family.

Aerosock's product positioning, according to Donna, is a somewhat difficult one. "I'll never be at the lowest price, and I tell people that. We lost the New Jersey DOT this year because we weren't the low bidder. I talked to the guy running the bid and he said, 'I know I'm going to hate the windsocks I'm buying, but this year the state budget is bad and I was told it had to be the low bid.' We sell quality, and I'll never be at the low price."

It seems, unfortunately for Donna, that the windsock bureaucrats are a bit more price sensitive than the fire chiefs who buy Charlie Genthner's hose.

Donna proceeded to list three key factors that contribute to a quality windsock. The nylon fabric needs a solvent, not water, coating. The fabric must be packed with dye and UV inhibitor, so it holds rich color while baking for months in the sun. Finally, the fabric has to be cut and sewn correctly to fit on the frame. While Donna cuts most of the fabric herself, maintaining a team of skilled seamstresses is essential to her success. As with most small business, it's not so much a matter of finding employees—Donna's challenge is finding the right employees.

"I supply all machines and materials and set the seamstresses up in their homes. I'm looking for people who want to work from home. Single mothers, people with sick relatives; there are quite a few people out there who would like to work but have circumstances that restrict them from working a traditional job. It is a certain type of person who wants to sit at a sewing machine and sew all the time. It's their niche, and I need to find them."

Paul noted, "So you're in for several thousand dollars between the machine and unfinished inventory at each seamstress location, right?" Donna nodded, and Paul continued. "So you have to pick seamstresses carefully and get people who are going to do a lot of work. Otherwise you have this expensive machine sitting idle."

"Absolutely," Donna quickly agreed and outlined her training regimen for new hires. "Each seamstress starts off here in the office. I give them scrap, and they have to sit and sew. After they can sew a straight seam, I'll give them real material, so they'll sew a windsock and I look at each one. If there's a problem, I rip the seams, we talk about the problems, and we start another one. A new seamstress has to learn the touch and control the speed. It's usually two weeks of working in the office before I'm comfortable thinking about sending them home."

"And how are people paid?" Scott asked.

"Our seamstresses are paid by the piece. We pay for what they produce. On a new seamstress, we measure every windsock before it is grommetted. Once they've been here a while, we visually inspect all of them and measure every third to fifth one. If it's wrong, it goes back to the seamstress to take it apart by hand and re-do it. New seamstresses often have to re-do maybe 30 percent, and the more you give them back, the better they get at it. I am very picky."

For Aerosock, a substandard employee would be a very costly burden. Not only is each employee sitting on thousands of dollars of machinery and inventory, but Donna has personally used two weeks of her own time in training. In addition, Donna's insistence on quality means that a sloppy seamstress is a slow seamstress; sloppy work will be caught and must be redone.

Aerosock solves this problem by using job design to induce self-selection. Specifically, these seamstress jobs are constructed so that the job is only attractive to the kind of person that Donna Lemmons wants.

The key elements of job design here are piecework compensation and Donna's insistence on quality. To see how the self-selection works, imagine what kind of experience a not-very-motivated seamstress would have going to work for Aerosock. If our not-so-motivated person is a skillful seamstress, then she can probably produce a good-quality windsock but won't produce very many of them. As a result of the by-the-piece pay, this person won't earn much and will probably be better off looking for another job where pay doesn't depend so much on the quantity of output.

If our not-so-motivated person is not a skillful seamstress, then she will be faced with a picky boss who keeps sending work back to be redone. This won't be good for self-esteem or take-home pay, so the seamstress had better increase her skill level quickly. A motivated seamstress will respond to this feedback and improve; a not-so-motivated person will, again, be better off looking elsewhere for work.

This dynamic plays itself out pretty quickly at Aerosock, often during initial interviews or the first few days of training. During our visit, Paul asked whether there are new hires who never make it past the in-office, two-week training. "Absolutely," Donna replied emphatically. "I had a new hire, in fact, who was here the last two days. She called this morning and isn't coming back. Usually if you can get them through the third or fourth day, you've got them."

There are three main steps to a self-selection hiring strategy. First, identify the characteristics that you're hoping to select on. That is, make a note of what type of person you're hoping to attract, and make a note of what type of person you're hoping to deter from applying. Second, structure the job so that it's unattractive to the type you're hoping to deter but attractive to the type you're hoping to attract. Third, make sure you're credibly communicating the relevant job characteristics as early as possible in the job-posting and interviewing process, so that you're deterring applications from the wrong types.

Self-selection is certainly no solution to all of Aerosock's hiring problems; Donna Lemmons reported feeling constantly understaffed and said she'd hire two additional seamstresses immediately if she could find them. Managers who implement a self-selection strategy often face a strong temptation to change job characteristics to try to fill vacancies. Donna could, for example, be less exacting during the first few days of training. Or she could modify her compensation plan to offer a modest hourly wage and a smaller piecework component. Doing so might help to get vacancies filled, but it's important to consider how these changes will affect the composition of her workforce. For Aerosock, changing job characteristics would mean hiring a marginal performer who would actually be worse for Donna than leaving the position unfilled.

Saint Joseph, Missouri
SAINT JOE DISTRIBUTING

Consider How Operations Skew Your Applicant Pool

Our time in Saint Joseph was, it turned out, quite rich in hiring examples. For our final stop of that ridiculously hot and humid day, we drove to an industrial park at the very eastern edge of town, just north of US 36. Big white trucks with an Indian headdress logo—is everything Wild West in this town?—filled the parking lot, and huge text on the trucks informed us that we had arrived at Saint Joe Distributing. Inside, we sat down with the company president, Brian Dickens.

In his late forties and trim, Brian greeted us wearing a gray suit, crisp white shirt, and red power tie. "We've been in business sixty-five years. I'm third-generation owner, and my daughter is fourth generation," he said from behind a massive wooden desk. A window behind his desk allowed a full view of the busy warehouse below.

"We're a wholesaler to convenience stores, and we ship to six states. A lot of our business revolves around cigarettes. Years ago, we really had three businesses: wholesale tobacco and candy, vending, and we also had a large retail showroom operation, selling jewelry and housewares. We divested vending and showroom and have focused on wholesaling since the late 1990s. To protect the candy and tobacco business, we had to evolve to be a full-service wholesaler to convenience stores. We do everything you'd see in a convenience store except for beer, Coke, and Pepsi."

Brian explained the core distribution tasks of receiving and picking as follows: "Essentially, we bring in big loads and break them down into smaller pieces for our customer. For example, we'll receive a full truckload of Mars candy and store it in our warehouse. When we get an order—say, two cartons of Skittles, three cases of M&Ms, six of something else—it goes to an employee who has to pick it. The employee goes through the warehouse, picks the items to fill the order, prepares it for shipping, and gets it to the truck. Our drivers take it from there."

"So you're really managing customers' inventory?" Mike asked.

"Exactly. It's a low-margin business, so they are watching every penny. It's funny. We added the convenience store products to keep customers coming to us for tobacco and candy, but the margins have really flipped there. Now we're doing well on things like snack cakes and ice cream, but the cigarettes…we can't do without 'em. If I didn't have the Marlboro Red, our customers would find another supplier."

"Altria, they're a sharp outfit. We hate 'em," Brian deadpanned.

Managing relationships—both upstream with suppliers and downstream with customers—is essential for Saint Joe's success. "Our customers are mostly independents and small chains. For probably 75 percent of our accounts, we have a sales rep there writing the order. That gives us some glue because the big companies"—Brian named a couple of his larger, national competitors—"say to the stores, 'You order.' We also spend a lot of money on technology, so our customers can easily see their orders, see what their inventory is, set things up to automatically order for them."

While Saint Joe deals with little guys on the downstream side, their suppliers, like Altria, are some of the largest companies in the world. "You also have to shine for these manufacturers. They want the best locations," Brian says. "We merchandise these stores, so we work with the owner to shift locations around. Sometimes a supplier will really want an end cap; for example, Jack Links with their meat snacks might pay two hundred dollars to get the right location, and I might give my salesman twenty dollars to make it work. Because of our strong sales force, the suppliers have to work through us to get good placement."

Like Aerosock, Saint Joe Distributing has made operational decisions with a clear eye on how it will affect their ability to hire the right workers. "We run about a sixteen- to eighteen-hour operation; we don't run a night shift," Brian explained. "I just came back from a share group with eleven other wholesalers across the country that we don't compete with, and they asked, 'How in the world, with that volume, do you do it five days a week during the day?'

"The key is we pick through the day. Distributors like us, mostly they receive early, get things put away, then start picking at five, six o'clock in the evening and run through the night. But we receive, put away, and pick during the day. There's a big overlap in hours across receiving and picking. We start receiving earlier than we pick, but we get it all done during the day."

Brian acknowledges that the overlapping receiving and picking times can lead to operational difficulties on the warehouse floor; imagine workers trying to pick but finding their path through the warehouse blocked by a forklift putting away a pallet of candy bars. Picking in a crowded warehouse is clearly less efficient, but, he argues, there's a hidden benefit of avoiding the night shift. "Our line workers start at $8.50 per hour. We've found our best workers are single moms with a couple of kids and a deadbeat ex-husband," he says. "If you run a night shift, they won't work for you. If you do run a night shift," he continues, "that's when you get the deadbeat ex-husbands here working. So if we can keep the hours for the moms, we get better workers. All this we've learned through our hiring mistakes."

Unlike Aerosock's, Saint Joe's hiring strategy does not cause employees to self-select. Recall that with a self-selection-based hiring strategy, the job is attractive to the type of worker the business wants, but unattractive to the type of worker it does not want. While it's clear that moms (the type that Saint Joe wants) prefer the day shift, it's probably the case that deadbeat ex-husbands (the type Saint Joe doesn't want) prefer the day shift as well.

Saint Joe's strategy of not running a night shift doesn't in-duce self-selection, but it does avoid an unfavorable "adverse selection." To understand this terminology, consider what Saint Joe's applicant pool looks like when it posts night-shift jobs. Moms really dislike these jobs and don't apply, while deadbeat ex-husbands probably dislike the jobs less and still ap-ply. The resulting applicant pool isn't a random selection of the potential applicant pool of moms and deadbeats; it's a se-lection that's more heavily tilted to deadbeats—and this is an adverse selection in the eyes of Saint Joe.

What are the implications of self-selection versus avoiding adverse selection? When hiring seamstresses, Donna Lemmons has to do little besides explain how the job works and allow those who are interested to come in for training. The employees she wants will stick it out, and the employees she doesn't want will quickly leave. Aerosock doesn't have to spend a lot of time screening, that is, trying to figure out—based on résumés and references—who's the right employee.

Saint Joe's strategy doesn't allow it to avoid screening, but it does make its screening problem a little easier. To see why, note that it's surely not the case that all ex-husbands are deadbeats, and this means that it would be possible for Brian Dickens to find a high-quality night-shift workforce. However, the ratio of needle to hay in the night-shift-willing population is pretty low, and this means that finding a high-quality night-shift workforce would be costly. Even if it put a lot of work into researching candidates, the company would probably still make a lot of costly hiring mistakes. By staying away from the night shift, Saint Joe's increases the needle-to-hay ratio—they can spend less time researching candidates and thus reduce the incidence of hiring mistakes.

Does it make sense for every business to adjust operations strategy to make hiring decisions easier? Probably not. But if hiring the right people is a crucial determinant of success for you, then it can pay to think carefully about how operations influence job design, which in turn influences the selection of people who apply for your openings.

After thanking Brian for the meeting, we walked slowly out of Saint Joe Distributing into a wall of moist heat, donning sunglasses and removing our coats before piling into the car. Our long, hot day in northwestern Missouri had finally drawn to a close.

"I feel bad for the divorced men of Saint Joseph," Mike said.
"No wonder some of them are late on the child support," Paul added. "Their ex-wives keep taking the job offers."

Scott nodded and cranked the AC. We cruised uneasily through the late afternoon sun, wondering if—or perhaps how often—our ex-wives referred to us as deadbeats.

Mazzeo's Law

The Right Hiring Strategy: What It Depends On

- **Screening Costs:** Hiring often requires a costly process of screening out hay to find an elusive needle. By playing hard to get—building in small hurdles that applicants must cross in order to be seriously considered—Southside Family Fun Center filtered out poor applicants and streamlined their process.

- **Productivity versus Wage:** Re Vera could have filled their vacancies at minimum wage, but paying more allowed them to attract productive employees, and this higher productivity more than offset the higher wage. The reverse is likely true at Southside Family Fun Center, where they've positioned themselves at the lower end of the wage/ability scale.

- **Self-Selection:** At Aerosock, Donna Lemmons was able to make the job unattractive to the wrong "type" of worker and therefore was able to get employees to self-select. Strong self-selection can greatly reduce or even eliminate screening costs.

- **Adverse Selection:** Saint Joe Distributing re-engineered their operations to avoid unfavorable adverse selection in hiring. For some businesses, hiring well is sufficiently important that it pays to view every operational decision with an eye on how changes might affect your ability to hire.

CHAPTER 8

Incentives for Employees

A midsummer trip happened to fall across Paul's birthday, so we asked for his guidance on where to celebrate.

"No chain restaurants. Let's find something that's authentic Middle America," he said. "Oh, and good beer. I might just have a second on my birthday."

Smartphone research revealed that one of Paul's favorite brews, Bass Ale, was on tap at the nearby Hi Ho Bar and Grill. We entered and found a dark, crowded bar with tables full of thirty-something couples, many still wearing softball jerseys from earlier co-ed rec-league games. Scanning the menu, we learned that while the Hi Ho is small, with seating for maybe fifty patrons, it has big dreams. A large graphic on the back announced: "Visit all of our locations nationwide!" and showed a map of the United States with a single red star, placed at our exact location.

"Should we leave them a draft of chapter 1 instead of a tip?" Scott asked after we toasted Paul with our first round. "Growth seems to be an issue."

"Their website says they've been here since 1910," Mike replied. "They've had time to try every growth strategy there is. Twice."

The Scrappy Beef Sandwich, which Paul ordered, is the house specialty. It's mostly notable, he said after not quite finishing it, for being just one typo away from the worst marketing strategy in the history of business.

"Should have asked for peanut butter on it," Mike said.

If dinner that night was a disappointment, dessert was not. Spending a summer evening with friends and dipped cones in a Dairy Queen parking lot is, we decided, about as good as it gets.

And while Scott's suggestion to stiff the waitress and leave behind management advice instead of a tip might have saved us a few dollars (and sold a few books), it would have been a serious problem for our friendly waitress. Federal minimum wage law specifies that "tipped" employees can be paid much less than the hourly minimum wage, which meant she was likely earning just $2.13 per hour. Her living, therefore, depended very much on the tips she was earning. If customers base their tips on the quality of service, then she faces a strong incentive to keep customers happy, which is probably just what the owners of the Hi Ho would want of her.

While customers take care of providing incentives to the waitstaff at bars and most restaurants, things are not so simple for most other businesses. All managers struggle at times with the problem of getting employees to take the right actions to move the company ahead, and employers use a strikingly wide range of strategies to combat this problem. Mazzeo's Law suggests that the right pay-for-performance strategy will depend

very much on the particulars of the incentive problems facing
your business.

Johnson City, Tennessee
EAGLE'S LANDING INFORMATICS

When Paying for Quantity, Don't Forget Quality

In Johnson City, Tennessee, we met Elisa Comer, owner of
Eagle's Landing Informatics. The company, which does medical transcription work, maintains a small office at the Ten
nessee Small Business Development Center, and Elisa arrived
carrying a large black purse and a supersized plastic cup filled
with ice water. She had come to our meeting from home
where, we learned, Elisa does most of her work. Indeed, the
desk and shelves in her "office" were almost completely bare
except for an old computer, a lone sheet of elementary-school
artwork, and a couple of photos of Elisa's kids.

"Our business is Internet-based," Elisa explained, "so our
people can be anywhere. Counting our clients and employees,
we're in sixteen states, Canada, and Chile. We all work from
home except for Chris—he's the technical guy and has to be
where the servers are."

Elisa, who is in her mid-forties and speaks with a mild
Southern accent, took an indirect route to this line of work.
"I have a nursing background, but I developed a severe latex
allergy. I couldn't take care of patients anymore. I got a cer-
tificate in medical transcription and stayed home, transcribed,

and took care of our children." Eventually she took over the business and has grown it to employ fifteen transcriptionists.

The task of transcription, Elisa explained, is straightforward. "The physicians dictate, the voice files are uploaded to our servers, and we turn it into structured text for their EMR [electronic medical records]."

While the task is straightforward, the training required to perform it well is anything but. "I have a training director who oversees the training and the hiring for me," Elisa said. "We've found those abbreviated, learn-it-real-fast training programs are insufficient for what transcriptionists—we actually call them medical language specialists now—really do. You can't learn medical anything in thirty days; there's just too much. So we've been partnering with the local colleges to be part of the solution."

Each day, doctors' offices in various locations upload recordings to Elisa's servers. When a transcriptionist logs on, he or she is assigned recordings on a first-come/first-served basis. The system is automated, so Elisa spends her time working with and selling to doctors and hospitals and hiring and managing transcriptionists.

Scott asked, "How do you pay your transcriptionists?"

"They are paid per line typed," Elisa explained. "They are paid some number of cents per line, based on the contract and the turnaround time. If they are working extra, they get a few cents more per line. They have to do at least eight hundred lines a day. If they've already done their eight hundred lines for the day and a doctor dumps on us and I need them to work a couple of extra hours, then I'll compensate them. It's kind of like overtime."

The key issue here is that Elisa (as the business owner) has different interests from her transcriptionist employees. While Elisa's primary concern is accurate transcription with a speedy turnaround time, her employees likely would prefer to be paid more but work less. Given this, Elisa would like to find some way to align the interests of the transcriptionists with her own interests—that is, she'd like to find a way to get her employees to work the way Elisa would if she were doing it herself.

If Elisa paid by the hour, her employees would probably type somewhat slowly. A transcriptionist, balancing pay versus workload, would see that putting in extra effort to speed through a physician's recording doesn't lead to any tangible benefit to him or her. That is, the employee's hard work is all cost but no benefit. By tying pay directly to an output-based performance measure, Elisa transforms the employee's cost/benefit calculation. Extra effort allows the employee to produce more lines in less time, which leads directly to extra pay. A transcriptionist will now balance the "cost" of hard work against the benefit of additional pay, and it becomes in the employee's interest—not just in Elisa's interest—for the employee to type faster. This plan aligns the interest of the employee with that of the business owner.

While this pay plan will give Elisa what she pays for—more lines—we worried about the side effects.

"Do you worry about accuracy?" Mike asked.

"Absolutely," Elisa said. "'Is' or 'Is not' is a big deal in medicine. 'The tumor WAS', 'The tumor WAS NOT'—there's a lot of liability for that. And the doctors are not always helpful by dictating at a normal speed. Some are speed demons and you have to hang in there."

To address this problem, Eagle's Landing employs a staff of quality assurance (QA) specialists to check on transcriptionists, especially those who have been hired recently. The QA team holds employees to exacting standards. "Very few of the people I hire initially make it through the training period to the point where the training director can stop giving them regular feedback. I would guess 20 percent or less make it," Elisa explains.

The presence of the Eagle's Landing QA staff points out an important potential limitation of pay-for-performance incentive plans. Elisa, as the owner, wants both speed and accuracy, but one way for transcriptionists to be faster is, of course, to skimp on accuracy. While her pay-by-the-line plan motivates speed, it may be directly counter to Elisa's accuracy goals, and this means she must carefully monitor quality to ensure that both of her goals are met.

Eagle's Landing thus provides an excellent example of the "it depends" of pay-for-performance incentive plans. Tying an agent's pay to some measure of performance can help align the interest of the employee with that of the owner. However, in most cases, the available measures of employee performance fail to capture some important aspects of performance. Tying pay to such measures will get you more of what you're paying for, but perhaps less of other things you value. It is crucial to think carefully through the properties of performance measures used in pay-for-performance plans.

Coeur d'Alene, Idaho
KLEIN'S DKI

Tailor the Measure to the Job

Companies often have a plethora of data and measures from which to choose when measuring an employee's performance. And in some cases, the difference between a great and a terrible incentive plan rests on picking the right measure.

We saw a great example of this when we visited Klein's DKI in Coeur d'Alene, Idaho, where we met with Rudy Klein, the proprietor and co-owner (with his wife Nancy). Klein's DKI does insurance restoration work and is a franchisee of DKI (Disaster Kleenup International).

Rudy, who has a large bald head and looks like he could have played linebacker thirty-five years ago, described the company's roots. "I was working for a guy in construction and we were living off of our savings account because he couldn't keep me busy. I told my wife that we could starve just as quick on our own, so in 1985, I started a remodeling company. I've always preferred the restoration stuff because, when the market goes down, there's still insurance work. I wanted to keep that up, and we ended up joining DKI."

Rudy's business is helping owners of businesses and homes after disaster strikes. A homeowner suffering water damage, for example, might call his insurance company, who then refers the homeowner to Klein's. Rudy sends a team to clean up the scene—get the water out of the house and dry out the walls, carpets, etc. Soon after, one of Rudy's estimators will put together a bid for the renovation work that is needed to get the house back to its original condition. Assuming the homeowner agrees, Rudy does the work and bills the insurance company.

Mike began by asking about Rudy's team. "Who are your key employees?"

Rudy responded by citing his marketing manager. "He goes out and takes ice cream and donuts to the insurance agents. He keeps our presence out there with the folks who refer us the business. Golf. Different things like that."

"Sounds pretty good," Scott said. "Are you hiring for that position?"

Paul, knowing that Scott can certainly knock back a few donuts but can't play golf, changed the subject. "How do you know if he's doing a good job? He's not a salesman. It's not like you can pay him by commission."

Turns out that Paul was wrong. Rudy countered, "He gets a salary and then he gets a percentage on anything that comes through the door from the agencies that he's calling on. We keep track of that."

"Does he pay for his own donuts?" Mike asked.

"No, we do," Rudy replied. "He's got a budget. He'll take an agency to lunch if he thinks that makes sense. Marketing people are notorious—you can't control them. You don't know where they are. You don't know what they have going."

Rudy's marketing manager is a bit like a work-from-home transcriptionist at Eagle's Landing Informatics. He needs to get out of the office to do his job properly, so Rudy cannot monitor his actions directly. How does Rudy get the marketing manager to do the things that Rudy would do if he held that job himself? How does he get him to aggressively court the insurance agents that will refer work to Klein's, and how does he get him to buy donuts and lunch for good potential customers rather than for his buddies?

The key to aligning the employee's interests with those of the company is to tie pay to some measure of performance. But what's the right measure? One alternative would be to connect the marketing manager's pay to the profit Rudy earns from the agencies the manager calls on. Profit is, after all, Rudy's end goal, so this may seem like a natural way to align interests. One problem with this approach, though, is that the marketing manager does not directly control the profitability of a job. He doesn't order materials, schedule work, or make sure things are getting done right the first time; the *cost side* of the profitability equation is beyond the marketing manager's control. Having worked hard to bring in work, the marketing manager would likely be very unhappy if operational errors wipe out the profits on a given job.

Rudy avoids that problem by paying the marketing manager based on the *revenues* he brings in—because that's what he controls. And he gives him a budget to spend knowing that he has the incentives to use that budget in the best interests of his revenue-based pay (and, as a result, of the company). Incentives work in this case because the manager is paid based on things that he can affect and that can be measured. This pay plan may not be perfect—the marketing guy may still play a bit more on-the-job golf than Rudy would if he were doing the job himself—but it goes a long way toward solving the natural tension between employee and employer.

Rudy next identified another important group of employees—his estimators. Good estimating, he says, is part science, part art. "There's a computer program that dictates the pricing based on an average for an area for different types of work. When you have software that you are working with and the insurance company is involved and you're trying to make a profit, you have to know that software inside and out. It's called being an artist."

If Rudy did all the estimating himself, he would try to price jobs to earn as much profit as possible, balancing the possibility of losing the business if he quotes too high against lower margins if he quotes too low. How can he get the estimators to think that way and to be thorough in their analysis? If he pays them by the hour, they may not spend enough time learning the details of the damage. This could lead to quotes that do not match the work to be done very well, so he might get a lot of customers who choose other contractors when his estimator bids too high and low-profit jobs when they bid too low.

While incentive pay makes sense, Rudy doesn't necessarily want to use the same incentive pay as he used for the marketing guys. As he pointed out, "The estimator has pricing latitude." So Rudy wants to be sure it is in the estimator's best interests to use that latitude in line with Rudy's best interests. If he pays them based on revenue, they would have an incentive to lowball on price and let Rudy deal with the fact that many jobs would then be unprofitable.

The result: "Estimators are paid on commission. It's based on profitability."

Rudy's experiences highlight the importance of tailoring the performance measure to the job when tying pay to performance. When selecting performance measures, it is beneficial to filter out factors that are beyond the control of the employee being evaluated.

Saint Joseph, Missouri
JR'S TBA

Know When Not to Use Pay-for-Performance

JR's TBA sits just east of downtown Saint Joseph, Missouri, a few blocks from the interstate and tucked just off the main drag. It's a white cinderblock building with some peeling paint and fading red lettering. A small sign, visible from the street, announces the name of the business and a short menu of services, which include tires, brakes, and alignments (TBA) and others. We pulled in on a busy weekday afternoon and parked our rental among the queue of cars waiting for service in the spacious lot.

The six bays were mostly full, with a mixture of foreign and domestic makes being worked on by a small team of men wearing matching red-and-white shirts with stitched name badges. The men glanced up but continued working as we walked past, nodding hello, and no doubt wondering about the three visitors in jacket and tie.

"Do they think we're bankers or accountants?" Paul asked.

"Tax inspectors, I bet," Mike quipped.

Walking into the small office, we were greeted by JR Cheek, a tall, slim man with a graying beard and thinning brown hair. JR spoke quickly and used locker-room language that made Paul blush. "We'll have to edit this transcript a bit," Scott thought after listening to JR's colorful descriptions of incidents involving his ex-wife and a troublesome neighbor.

JR was encouraged by his first employer, the owner of a local junkyard, to become a mechanic. "'Hey, you got mechanical ability. Why don't you pursue it? Don't be like me and get stuck here,' he told me. So I went to a vocational school, worked my way through, got into sales at a tire store, and the next thing you know I'm running a store."

A few years later, he opened JR's TBA on a shoestring. "I had no money for advertising. But I had the phone number of the garage that was here before," JR recalled. Customers would call up, expecting the previous owner, and JR would get them to come in and counted on word-of-mouth from there.

JR started using pay-for-performance with his first employee, another mechanic. "I made sure that he was compensated. I guaranteed some and gave him a flat share of what he did. The harder he worked, the more he got rewarded. As long as I had the work, he got it. It kept rolling, and there's six of us now."

JR explained that this approach continues to work well with his lead technician. "I pay the lead technician by the job. If the job calls for an hour of labor and he does it in thirty minutes, he gets an hour of pay. He's cranking out the work. The more cars he can work, the more money he makes. He is my bread and butter. You throw that technician a job, stand back because that guy wants to work. He pays the bills around here."

This pay scheme gets the technician to work in a way that is close to the way JR would work if he were doing it himself. Because JR can measure the technician's output (jobs completed), the technician is similar to an Eagle's Landing transcriptionist. Once JR is sure he can trust the technician not to skimp on quality, JR can use pay based on output to align his interests with those of the mechanic.

One important aspect of JR's business is uncovering opportunities for additional repairs when employees are working on cars. JR described a hypothetical scenario with one of his employees: "Say a customer comes in for an oil change, and the tech does an oil change. I'm not here to rob anybody, but the tech should put your car up in the air. Once it's in the air, what does he see? He's working on the oil but he can check one brake. He should check pressure in all the tires as a courtesy and maybe he'll feel something loose. He might uncover a want or a need that you have. If he asks for that order, that's where I become profitable."

"I have to train the guys to do that," JR continued. "They think, 'Why would I do that? I can do this repair quicker if I don't.' But I want guys to be thorough. I want them to uncover those wants and needs so I can go to the customer and say, 'Hey—you got a loose tie rod.' I get an alignment out of the deal. Maybe a tire. If you train them to do their job appropriately when your back is turned, you got it made."

Based on this description, we expected that JR could align interests by paying employees a commission based on the additional revenue arising when employees find "wants and needs." It turns out, however, that JR did not have good luck with such a plan. Employees, he found, focused too much on uncovering wants and needs, creating an incentive to do a hard sell on the customer, or worse, to suggest unnecessary repairs. This led to unhappy customers, which JR believed cost him more in the long run. The wants-and-needs commission failed to align interests because it encouraged employees to think too much about the short run and not enough about the long-term value of the customer.

This example raises an important point about pay-for-performance incentives. Sometimes tying pay to a poor measure of performance is worse than simply relying on hourly pay and direct monitoring. In JR's case, the incentive plan led to some of what he wanted—uncovering wants and needs—but too much of what he didn't want—suggestions for unnecessary repairs. It is essential to think hard about exactly what actions (positive and negative) will be motivated by the use of a given performance measure. If tying pay to a poor measure yields more cost than benefit, then find another measure, or unlink pay and performance entirely. While JR pays his lead technician by the job, other employees remain hourly, in large part because he's concerned they will sacrifice too much quality for speed.

"Why the video system?" Paul asked, referring to the bank of monitors behind JR's desk, linked to cameras in the garage.

"To discourage employee theft," JR replied. "Parts theft could be a problem, but I do trust all my guys on that. But then there is theft of time. When the boss is away, I don't want them sitting on their asses."

Because of the limitations of his output-based measures of employee performance, JR monitors the employee's "inputs" directly by video. This yields a stick approach—reprimanding or firing employees who repeatedly misbehave—as opposed to the carrot of pay-for-performance incentives.

Cincinnati, Ohio
PLASTIC MOLDINGS COMPANY

Use Group Pay to Drive Common Goals

North of Eaton, Ohio, we turned off US 127 and came upon a large 1970s rambler-style house with rustic wood exterior siding and vaulted ceilings. "Are we staying with my parents?" Scott grumbled, having grown up in just such a house in suburban Portland, Oregon.

"Welcome to the Whispering Oaks Bed & Breakfast!" announced Paul, having arranged this night's lodging.

"B&B owners always want to *talk* to you," Scott snarled. "I hate that."

Inside, the friendly proprietor showed us to our upstairs bedrooms. "There are two bedrooms down this hallway, and one over there," she said, smiling. "The bathroom is here."

Mike panicked, scarred by distant memories of his *own* childhood home, in which he shared a bathroom with his three sisters. "Just the one bathroom?" he asked. "For all three of us?"

As Scott and Paul played 8-Ball and drank beer from cans in the rec room, Mike stayed upstairs to plot strategy. "First awake is first to the bathroom," he figured, "Paul's usually up at 6:00. But he'll be fifteen minutes early to try to beat me, so I have to be up fifteen minutes before that...5:30 it is."

Paul woke at 6:00, went for a quick run, showered, and found Mike waiting at the kitchen table. Breakfast was a rich quiche casserole, which, Mike guessed, contained double the calories and quadruple the cholesterol of his normal weekly diet. The meal was rich in conversation as well, as our hostess grinningly peppered the two with questions about our upcoming day.

"You look terrible," Paul said to Mike, as our hostess excused herself to fetch more scones for the table. "Sleep OK?"

"A little stuffy in my room," Mike replied, unwilling to admit that his scheming had led to insomnia.

Meanwhile, Scott outsmarted them all, staying in bed until well after both had showered and breakfast had been cleared. He grabbed a quick coffee, tersely thanked the hostess, and we were on our way.

Later that day, we met with Thom Gerdes, CEO of Plastic Moldings Company (PMC), at his office on the outskirts of Cincinnati. PMC manufactures plastic components, mostly for tier-one automobile suppliers and, increasingly, medical equipment makers.

The company's headquarters occupy about 4,000 of the 60,000 square feet in the facility where PMC once manufactured. They now do the production at a factory eighty-five miles away in Shelbyville, Indiana, and at a joint venture facility in Mexico, so most of the Cincinnati space sits empty. A mustached wiry man of about sixty, Thom—who looks like a young Walter Matthau, or a gentle Charles Bronson— explained the business as we sat at a round conference table in his office.

"Our business is technical manufacturing," he began. "The common thread is plastics, but our markets have evolved over the years. In our recent history, we have been primarily in the automobile industry, particularly in underhood engineering applications.

"We've also developed a medical devices business. Our technology is high-heat, esoteric materials that are uniquely qualified to be implanted during surgery. Some of these high-heat materials are self-lubricating, they're durable, and they're nontoxic. As an example, we make suture anchors for soft-tissue repair in shoulders, elbows, and knees."

Thom told us how he came to lead the family business. "My involvement was not by plan. I was the first in my family to graduate from college, and I got engaged at the end of my junior year at the University of Cincinnati. I was thinking seriously of going to law school, but I needed to make some money. It was shortly after *The Graduate* had come out, so people were always quoting the famous advice to Dustin Hoffman to go work in 'plastics.'"

Since taking over the company, Thom has slowly and steadily responded to the market forces that have thwarted so many American manufacturers. While PMC's products were commoditized when he got into the business, the product line has steadily gotten more advanced and differentiated. "Our business is *technical* manufacturing. Our magic dust is the process technology," he said.

Even with this specialization, Thom explained, the companies he supplies drive a very hard bargain. "Because of the sophistication of the purchasers, the negotiated contracts often have price-downs built in. We know going in that we are going to have to reduce costs by two or two and a half percent a year."

"It is like day-to-day, hand-to-hand combat." Thom ruefully described the pressure from his customers. "It's very difficult."

Given these tough negotiations and the future price reductions they have agreed to, it is absolutely essential for PMC to continue to generate manufacturing cost savings while making their cutting-edge products. How do they do it?

Thom reported that incentive bonuses, which run about 7 percent of monthly pay for production workers, are a big part of the story. "The guys on the line are on a shared incentive based on global cost measurement. Our people suggest lots of different ways to reduce cost—running faster, 'lean' activities, changing a material, utilization of space. The plan is plant wide for the 150 people who work there. The workers at the plant get 50 percent of any savings that are generated."

Paying workers for cost reductions makes perfect sense for PMC—otherwise, the company wouldn't be able to afford the contractual discounts. But we were initially skeptical of his team-based, rather than individual-based, pay-for-performance system. PMC wants employees to think hard about ways to cut costs, but it's unclear how strong the incentives associated with this plan would be. To see why, think about an innovative PMC employee who comes up with an idea that can save, say, $3,000. If that idea is implemented, the employees at the plant get $1,500. With 150 workers at the plant, however, the innovator's share is only $10; the other $1,490 goes to his co-workers. An innovative employee may decide it's not worth the trouble to push new ideas. Because the benefits arising from any individual's action are shared with all, employees reduce effort and try to "free-ride" on the efforts of others.

Despite this potential free-rider problem, other factors can make team-based pay better than individual-based incentives. First, it can make sense to tie pay to a team's output when interaction among workers is productive. The example above imagines a single worker coming up with a cost-saving idea, but in PMC's case, it appeared that the best cost-saving innovations happened when employees worked together. "It's not a silver bullet, but little incremental improvements" that were most rewarding, according to Thom.

A second reason to use group-based pay is "mutual monitoring." While JR chooses to monitor his workers himself (with cameras in the garage) to keep them motivated, PMC's group-pay plan provides incentives for workers to watch over each other, saving managerial costs. "Some people are highly motivated because that's who they are," Thom reports about his employees. The team-based incentive plan gives them something else to do—encouraging their co-workers to be more productive.

Keeping the bonus top-of-mind is critical for the team-based plan, Thom says. "They receive the bonus monthly. It's all measured and displayed graphically so everyone can track it as it goes along."

For now, Thom says, "This is the best incentive we have ever had at the factory." But the free-rider arithmetic gets more problematic as companies grow and the gains from innovation are shared among a larger group. A group of 150 employees is already pretty big and, if the PMC factory grows, the company will have to think about whether to tailor specific incentives to smaller segments of the factory.

Council Bluffs, Iowa
STUART TINLEY LAW FIRM

Pay Based on Subjective Assessments When Objective Measures Are Imperfect

The Stuart Tinley Law Firm can trace its history of practicing law in Council Bluffs, Iowa, over 150 years. It now consists of six attorneys (none of whom are named Stuart or Tinley) and a handful of support staff that do paralegal and administrative work. We met with Gary Faust, a partner at Stuart Tinley, in a small concrete office building in downtown Council Bluffs. A large man in his sixties—another former linebacker, we suspect—Gary led us to tall leather chairs around a heavy wooden table in the firm's second-floor conference room.

"This firm has traditionally been a full-service firm," Gary began. "Part of what we do is my bailiwick, which is estates, trusts, and conservatorships. We also do transactional work, real estate, and some corporate—LLCs and the like. Other partners practice in personal injury and wrongful death, and another represents some school districts. We touch on most areas of the law."

As we listened, Scott wondered why this group of attorneys was working together. "Why it is useful for you to be in this firm instead of operating as a sole practitioner?" he asked.

"If someone comes in with an estate question, my partners can refer it to me," Gary responded. "If someone is involved in an automobile accident, I can refer that to them. There are limits, though. One of my partners does some criminal work.

I don't refer a lot of clients to him because my clients are not the type that get involved in crime. They are aghast if they get a ticket."

Paul, who had two teenage drivers at home, thought about how he might export some ticket-anxiety back to California.

To operate successfully, Stuart Tinley must provide incentives for its lawyers to undertake numerous tasks. Partners must, of course, do legal work because the firm bills clients by the hour. But the firm also needs its partners to search for opportunities to refer business to others. Administrative work, like managing office staff, is needed to keep the operation running efficiently. Finally, the firm wants its lawyers to improve its image and visibility by serving in community organizations and legal industry groups.

How can the firm use incentive pay to ensure that lawyers perform activities that add value? The firm could tie an attorney's pay to his or her billable hours since this figure contributes most directly to profits. This would likely discourage all other activities, though, since time spent on these other activities would be time taken away from billings.

The firm could also try to measure and reward other activities directly by, for example, paying a commission for the number of community organizations the partner works with. This would likely encourage too much time taken away from billings; you might imagine partners signing up for every community organization in Council Bluffs if they are paid simply for participation.

Finally, the partners could simply split the firm's profits six ways, but this would weaken the incentive to generate billable hours. A partner's effort to generate an additional $600 in billings for the firm would result in just $100 for the partner who did the work.

The ideal pay scheme at Stuart Tinley would appropriately reward all the different ways a partner might add value. It would align the interests of an individual partner with those of his or her partners. As the foregoing discussion shows, however, it's difficult to accomplish this using a numerical formula that ties pay to various measures of performance.

Gary explained how Stuart Tinley addresses this difficult problem. "There are a few 'eat what you kill' firms around here. We don't operate in that manner. We have a true partnership. Around the first of the year, we sit down and determine percentage ownership for the coming year. A lot of that is based on the income that a partner brought in, but there are other factors.

"There is some recognition within the firm for your contributions such as activity in the community—I was on the community college board, I serve as the chair of the library foundation, and some other things—and for doing some of the things nobody wants to do. Nobody in a law firm wants to spend time on the finances, the improvements of the office, and the HR function."

In real time, the partners meet and look over the objective data on hours billed and discuss the softer contributions such as administrative work, community work, and referrals. They complement the objective criteria with subjective information.

Mike imagined the scene. "So, first of the year, everybody gets into a room—this room, maybe? That must be an interesting meeting."

Gary smiled. "There can be some spirited conversation. The partnership's chemistry right now is good. At one point, it was a little bit acrimonious—especially when there were older partners who were not providing as much income, or even assistance. But they viewed themselves as rain makers, and thought, 'You young punks need to understand that if it weren't for me, clients wouldn't be coming in.' That can cause some real issues in law firms."

You might not immediately think of good "chemistry" as a key ingredient of a pay-for-performance plan, but here partners' relationships are critical to the success of Stuart Tinley's compensation system. Once the firm commits to using softer, qualitative measures, it is essentially agreeing that if a partner does his share and pulls his weight, he will be compensated for it. Each partner has to trust that the other partners will honor that implicit agreement and that they will all be able to agree on what is valuable; otherwise, it will be impossible to come to a resolution on a fair division of profits. In that case, the firm would have to switch back to relying on objective measures. While that would make splitting the spoils of the firm's success easier, it would not motivate all the actions that would maximize those spoils in the first place.

Meetings in a conference room when splitting the year's income can be difficult and potentially acrimonious. But they may be the best way to manage the trade-off between providing incentives to work hard and to also spend time doing things for the greater good of the company when it is impossible to measure all these things objectively.

Gary's story also highlights one of the advantages of being a small firm. A huge law firm with hundreds of partners can't realistically have the kind of meeting around a conference table that Stuart Tinley can. Such a firm may be forced to have a more formulaic way of allocating its income, which could lead to misaligned incentives. Being small, Stuart Tinley can more easily incorporate subjective information into its pay plan, and it is in a better position to build the trust and chemistry needed to implement such a plan.

After handshakes with Gary, we crossed the Missouri River and headed for the airport. On the way, we identified several ways that our own partnership suffered from incentive problems.

"You'd be Elisa Comer's worst transcriptionist," Paul said to Scott. "We should pay you by the line so your chapter drafts won't be so late."

"Maybe in donuts," Mike added, nodding.

"If you pay for quantity, you'll surely be sorry when my exquisite prose turns monosyllabic," Scott replied. "How about instead we fire anyone who books us a shared bathroom?"

Mazzeo's Law

Providing Good Incentives for Employees: What It Depends On

- **Quality:** If you pay an employee based on the quantity he or she produces, you're likely to get more output at the expense of quality. Eagle's Landing Informatics combines its per-line-typed incentive system with significant investments in quality control.

- **Performance Measurement**: An incentive pay plan is only as good as the measure used to track performance. Klein's DKI carefully tailors the performance measure to the job in order to align the employees' interests with those of the company, while JR's TBA relies on direct monitoring and hourly pay when the available measures of performance are not sufficiently good.

- **Team Size and Group Interaction**: Team-based incentives can be effective when you want to motivate cooperative behavior, when it is hard to identify individual contributions, and when the team size is not too big. PMC drives its incremental process improvement goal by rewarding its whole factory for the cost savings the workers identify collectively.

- **Subjective Assessments**: In some cases, hard data on performance is difficult to obtain, and companies can provide better incentives by making subjective assessments of performance. This approach requires that employees will trust the employer's promise to pay for good work when it is observed.

CHAPTER 9

Delegation

Throughout most of our Roadside MBA travels, Scott was serving a three-year term—or "sentence," as he called it—as associate dean at the University of Utah's School of Business. In this role, he was overseeing most of the school's degree programs, including the undergraduate and full-time MBA, and he happened into this work at precisely the wrong time. The Great Recession of 2008–2009 put immense pressure on public universities as state funding fell, tuition rose, and students flooded into the classrooms as a refuge from the lousy job market.

This meant, unfortunately, that Scott couldn't exactly disconnect when we were out on the road. Unlike your typical college professor, deans have actual responsibilities even though, in a world of employed-for-life tenured professors, they have little real power. And this led to some pretty hilarious (for Paul and Mike) phone calls.

Expecting a call, Scott rode in the front passenger seat as Paul steered through Rolla, Missouri, on our way to Jefferson City.

"This is Scott."

(Pause)

"Whoa, calm down. Deep breath..."

(Pause)

"Chairnapping? Um, what does that mean?"

(Pause)

"Did he say why he needs the chairs right now?"

(Pause)

"Look, I'm not happy about the, uh, chairnapping, but did you have to scream at him in front of the whole staff?"

This went on for a good fifteen minutes as Scott slowly talked one of his direct reports off the office-furniture warpath. He eventually clicked his phone to end the call, stared out at the evening shadows, and gave the unhappiest-sounding sigh ever.

"What happened?" Mike asked.

"We're halfway through construction on a new building, and everybody is displaced due to some recent teardowns. One of my teams just moved into the moldy basement of a 1950s building, and apparently the chairs that were down there actually belonged in another, newer building. My team was already feeling put-upon, and then the manager of another department waits until I'm out of town, and pulls rank to grab their chairs."

"Are we talking fancy Herman Miller desk chairs?" Paul asked.

"Not even. In each office, there's a desk, a desk chair, and then a couple of chairs for visitors to sit on. The chairnapping involved the visitor chairs."

Paul and Mike sat silently for a moment, pondering the

ridiculousness of it all, and then Mike ventured some unsolicited advice. "Scott, you're the associate dean. Shouldn't you be focusing on the broad strategic issues? Why isn't the Great Utah Chair Heist somebody else's job?"

"You'd be shocked at the minutiae I spend time on," Scott said. "When you're in charge, anything that isn't specifically somebody else's job lands on you, and it's easy to get bogged down. Plus, we have no admin staff to delegate to—we're struggling to invest in basic student services."

"I recall advising you not to take that job," Paul needled as Scott rolled his eyes and sighed unhappily again.

While we didn't hear many stories as dumb as Chairgate, Scott's dilemma was echoed by dozens of businesspeople we talked to out on the road. Mazzeo's Law says that "empowering" your employees can sometimes be the right strategy, but at other times, "If you want something done right, you have to do it yourself." Delegating effectively requires deep thinking about whether subordinates will make good decisions, and this means delegation and incentives issues are often very tightly linked. It's a hard problem that requires a careful and constant balancing act, and we found several smart tactics that can help businesspeople manage these trade-offs.

Jefferson City, Missouri
MIDWEST PRODUCTS GROUP

Delegate When Information and Incentives Align

Our visit to Midwest Products Group the next day had the misfortune of following a heavy lunch at the Jefferson City Country Club. We were ready for a nap.

"Can you remind me what this company does?" Paul asked as we stopped for coffee on our way back into town. "I'm guessing they make some kind of product and are based here in the Midwest."

"Midwest Products' main business is Midwest Block & Brick. They make concrete blocks," Scott replied. "The kind of thing you'd see as the outer facade of a new school or condo building."

"Concrete or cement?" Paul asked. "I always forget which is which." (Paul is pretty good on presidents, less so on building materials.)

Mike chimed in with "Cement is the ingredient in concrete that binds it all together."

"Right, so Midwest Block & Brick buys cement and uses it to make concrete blocks," Scott said.

"Oh boy," Paul moaned, turning toward the barista. "Can I get an extra shot of espresso in that?"

Back in the car, we made our way to a nondescript four-story office building just a few blocks from where the State Capitol overlooks the Missouri River. Midwest Products Group's office had the feel of a recent renovation, with dark

wood, tan walls, and newish furniture that Scott's staff would
have killed for. We stated our business and waited briefly while
a receptionist summoned CEO Pat Dubbert. A big man in his
early fifties with a mustache and a full head of dark hair, Pat
greeted us with a handshake and then led the way to a small
conference space adjacent to his office.

"I got started as a cement salesman," Pat began, in a gravelly
monotone that made Paul take a big hit of his Starbucks extra-
shot. "I liked sales, but I wanted to get into management and
have some ownership. In 1983, I found an opportunity to buy
part of a block plant here in Jeff City. It was something I could
afford to get into, and I thought there was a chance to expand
it. We did half a million in sales and had ten employees when
I bought in, and in 2006 we were right at ninety-five million
and had 380 employees."

Paul snapped awake as he mentally averaged this out to a
25 percent annual growth rate in sales, maintained for twenty-
plus years. This was no sleepy contractors' supply house.

Pat described a series of acquisitions over a period of years
that left the company with a large geographic footprint. "In
Missouri, we have block plants in Saint Louis, Kansas City,
Springfield, and Jefferson City. Then we have Paducah, Kentucky; Union City, Tennessee; Springfield, Illinois; and we just
got a nice deal on a plant in Springdale, Arkansas. It's uneco-
nomical to transport block more than about a hundred miles,
so the Springdale plant will allow us to get into the Tulsa
market."

While one company's concrete block isn't much different
from another's, Midwest Block & Brick maintains command-
ing market shares in all its locations, and the pursuit of scale

economies is a big part of the story. "Most every location we're in, we've got a majority of the market," Pat reported. "In this business, it's hard to make it when you only have one plant or maybe two. Here in the central office, we do our HR, accounting, IT, purchasing, and marketing. If you're small, you still need all those people, and so we get a lot of synergies from combining the plants."

Midwest Block's business model features two conflicting imperatives. First, the manufacturing has to be dispersed geographically due to transport costs; one megaplant in Jefferson City would simply not be competitive with smaller plants located at hundred-mile intervals. Second, the business needs to centralize certain activities in order to achieve economies of scale. This mix of centralization and decentralization presents a management challenge for Pat, and we turned there next.

"What are the sorts of things you want plant managers to be doing?" Paul asked. "And how do you keep track of what's going on in all your plants? They're spread out all over."

"Plant managers oversee production, inventory, and sales within their area," Pat replied. "And I also want them talking to customers. As far as keeping track, we have an executive meeting here every six weeks, and I also travel around to all the locations. If I go to Saint Louis for two or three days, for example, I go have lunch with customers, then I'll hang around the office a bit, maybe walk around the plant. I try to visit all of our locations at least every two months, maybe once a month for our bigger plants. We've also got plants set up as individual profit centers."

Pat delegates certain decisions to take advantage of dispersed local knowledge. Compared to Pat, local plant managers have easier access to information about customers—mostly local contractors—and are in a better position to match the block plant's production to local inventory and local customer demands. Plus, there are no significant economies of scale associated with these activities; calling ten customers in Springfield, Missouri, doesn't make it less costly to then call ten more customers in Springfield, Illinois, so there would be little to gain from centralizing sales at the home office.

When delegating, however, it's never enough to think just about who has information that is useful for making good decisions; it's essential to also think about that decision maker's incentives to make good choices. Pat's ideal would be for plant managers to use their information—things that he, as CEO, does not know—to make exactly the decision that he would make if he had that information. As one example, note that profit maximization requires that production scheduling be responsive to customer needs. Some customers may have needs that are truly time sensitive, and a profit-motivated owner might find it worthwhile to rearrange existing production schedules to serve that customer. This is information that would be very difficult for a distant CEO to get, but it might also be difficult to get a salaried manager to act upon this information in the value-maximizing way. Tying pay to plant-level profits generates incentives for plant-level managers to use their local knowledge to make good decisions. And this means Pat Dubbert can delegate big decisions to plant managers and be reasonably confident in the choices these managers will make.

While this organizational structure facilitates delegation and keeps many decisions off the CEO's desk, Pat cannot simply sit home in Jefferson City and watch the profits pile up. We asked what he's looking for when he travels.

"I do try to get to know the employees because I'm the one who finalizes any pay raises or promotions," Pat said. "I go through four hundred or so performance reviews a year."

"But each manager runs a profit center, and making good HR decisions is important for profits. Why don't you delegate that?" Mike wondered.

Pat thought for a few seconds, then responded: "Usually I'll tell my managers what we're looking at for raises in a given year; maybe we can do 3 percent. Then most of the managers recommend the standard raise, pretty much across the board. They don't ever want to try to cut anybody out of anything. But not everybody deserves a raise each time, and I'll tell my managers 'You can't tell me everybody's doing a great job and they all deserve the same raise.'"

Pat's refusal to delegate pay and promotion decisions points out one limitation of profit centers. In making decisions, employees weigh benefit versus cost. At Midwest Block, the benefit to a plant manager of making good decisions—whether operational or HR—comes from the resulting impact on plant-level profit, and thus on performance evaluation for the plant manager. However, the cost side matters too, and for Pat's managers the benefit of differentiating between good and bad performers isn't large enough to offset the fact that telling an employee, "No, you didn't earn a raise this year," is quite unpleasant. Pat is therefore concerned that his managers will have too few difficult conversations, and as a result he chooses not to delegate these important decisions.

There is an important managerial distinction between production planning and employee performance reviews at Midwest Block & Brick. Plant managers, who are in constant contact with both customers and employees, have easier access to relevant information for both decisions. Information is, however, only half the story. While the profit-center-based incentives are strong enough to motivate good operational decisions, they are not strong enough to motivate good choices on difficult HR decisions. Thus, the incentives side of the equation leads Pat Dubbert to make different delegation choices for these two seemingly similar decisions.

Athol, Idaho
SILVERWOOD THEME PARK

Ponder the Pitfalls of Accounting Profits as a Performance Measure

While profit centers can facilitate delegation by encouraging employees to think through the profit consequences of their actions, it's almost never possible to devise a perfect measure of an employee's (or a group of employees') contribution to overall value. We saw a great example of this off US 95 in northern Idaho, where we were treated to the remarkable story of the Silverwood Theme Park, which was bootstrapped as a second career by computer entrepreneur Gary Norton, and is now Idaho's largest tourist destination, with more than sixty rides and attractions spread over four-hundred-plus acres.

Finding our way to the staff entrance, we met Paul Norton, Gary's son and the park's general manager. He used the walkie-talkie system to locate Gary, and we met inside the park's Victorian Coffee House. Unlike his son, Gary was not dressed in the standard Silverwood uniform of a blue short-sleeve button-down with a logo and a name badge, choosing instead a plaid shirt with jeans. With thinning gray hair and a robust tan, he could have passed for an early-retiree grandpa of any kid in the park. And as Gary began his story, we quickly realized that— yet again—we were not the smartest guys in the room.

"I started a computer business when I was twenty-nine," Gary began. "It was right when microprocessors first came out, so I built a banking terminal and talked some S&Ls into trying it. It was a fun quick-growth story; we grew it to a couple hundred million in sales and went public in three years. But I got bored with running it after a while and sold out.

"My hobby at the time was old airplanes, and I ended up buying this little airport on the property where Silverwood now sits. Then, one day, I was at an airplane auction in Reno when a 1915 steam engine came up. I fell in love with it, brought it back here, and tried to figure out what to do with it. We put tracks through the woods and started selling tickets, and that was the start of Silverwood. It was not exactly a business plan, more of a fun plan. It's a really dumb thing to do, to try to build a theme park in north Idaho."

Gary went on to describe how he lost significant sums in his first few years of train rides and eventually figured he'd either have to "walk away or go for it." Gary went for it. He began buying theme-park rides from bankrupt parks in the East, which he personally took apart and reassembled on-site. He grew into a theme-park renaissance man, writing all the park's computer software, drawing up plans for new rides, designing the sewers, and even programming the lighting board for a winter ice-skating show. Gary—an incredibly high-energy guy who doesn't mind sweating the details—slowly pulled Silverwood out of the red and then began generating healthy returns.

The park's current strategy is still greatly influenced by its bootstrap history. "The way the park was structured and built, I never planned on getting the attendance we get now," Gary said. "When you put twelve thousand people in here like we did on Saturday, it's shoulder-to-shoulder."

"The wait for the Tremors coaster, the big wood one, was an hour and a half all day Saturday," added Paul.

"I can't grow revenue by growing attendance," Gary continued. "I have to increase per-cap spending. So I've really had to make it more of a boutique park with quality that's way past expectations. It's the only way to justify charging more."

"Can you give us an example of 'quality way past expectations' and how you manage for that?" Scott asked.

Gary nodded. "I was visiting another park, and I went into their ice cream store—virtually nobody there. In our ice cream store, you're going to stand in line all day, and the difference is that we overscoop. A few years back, I hired a new general manager, and first thing he did was cut costs for me by $600,000. Trouble is, for the next four years, we were trying to get our customers to come back and buy food in the park. What I've found is that people in management looking at profit reports don't understand that if you cut the cost of your burgers, somebody out there isn't going to like it. They may not say anything to you, but over time your sales are going to decline."

This story illustrates a common problem with "profit" as a measure of performance. Accounting profit, defined as this year's revenue minus this year's cost, is inherently a short-term number, but in many cases an employee's actions can affect both short-run profits and long-run value. At Silverwood, the new manager boosted short-run profits by cutting cost— perhaps by telling employees to stop it with the overscoops— but hurt long-run value because customers, over time, noticed the change in quality. Owners, like Gary Norton, care about long-run value, but employees typically have shorter time horizons. This means that tying employee pay to accounting profits can encourage them to think too much about the short-run effects of their decisions.

Because incentives and delegation issues are so tightly linked, this difficulty with providing the right incentives means difficulty with delegating these decisions. Recall that an owner's ideal would be for subordinates to use their information to make exactly the decision that the owner would make in that situation. Here, tying pay to accounting profits helps provide incentives for food and beverage managers to work hard, but it may also cause managers to skimp on quality.

And this fact explains Gary's plaid shirt. "I do not ever go out in a uniform," he said. "Guests don't know I own the park, so I just stand back and listen to them."

His son Paul, the general manager, laughed. "And he lets me know how they're doing."

"I'm the detail auditor," Gary said, flashing a big grin.

Blending in with the Silverwood crowd gives Gary a direct pipeline to customer-satisfaction data—much better than he could ever get with an email survey—and alerts him to quality problems before they get out of hand. Doing this, however, takes up a lot of Gary's time. Because of the limitations of profits as a measure of employee performance, it's probably not possible for Gary Norton to get food and beverage completely off his plate (so to speak).

Middletown, Ohio
BERNS GARDEN CENTER

Spot Externalities and Keep Senior Management Involved

The tension between short and long term is but one of a number of potential problems with using accounting profits as a part of a delegation strategy. We saw an example of another problem at Berns Garden Center. It was a cool late-April afternoon, and the southwestern Ohio planting season was about to swing into high gear. We parked out front and wandered into the store, which was packed to the rafters with lush greenery. Mike Berns, rotund with a gray beard, tinted glasses, and an easy-going, bantering sense of humor, led us to his office in the back.

Paul began our interview. "It seems like gardening might be a somewhat crowded retail space. Why do customers choose Berns?"

"We're faaaabulous," Mike B. said, drawing out the first syllable for effect. "When a potential customer thinks plants, we want her thinking, 'Oh, I'll go to Berns. I loooove that place.' Pretty corny... but that's what we want."

"And what makes customers loooove it?" Paul asked, mimicking Mike B.'s dramatic delivery.

"We have a beautiful facility, open and airy with plenty of parking. Easy to get to. And we have a great retail crew. They're very knowledgeable, but customers mostly like our people because they said, 'Oh, what a pretty dog you have.' Or 'I like your glasses.' We build a personal relationship because we want the customer to come buy from us for twenty years."

Scott, perplexed, asked, "How do you get your sales team to compliment somebody's dog?"

"We tell them to do that," Mike B. replied patiently.

"I tell my employees stuff all the time, and they ignore me," Scott muttered half to himself, as he thought back to the Great Utah Chair Heist and his widely disregarded directive not to send accusatory late-night emails to co-workers.

Mike B. continued. "We hire a lot each spring, and it's the song-and-dance people we keep through the winter. Our people are actors on a stage; I want themed employees who look like a character. One's tall and gruff, and some customers like that. Another's a sweet old lady who loves your dog."

Scott pondered this idea, imagining both the impact of themed lecturers on students and the reaction of staid professors when instructed to choose between a "tall and gruff" or "sweet old lady" persona.

Berns is a family business, started by Mike B.'s parents more than a half-century ago, and he and his two brothers comprise the top management team. "Each brother runs a division," he explained. "Greg runs the production greenhouses, Jeff does the landscaping division, and I oversee our two retail stores in addition to being the general manager for the entire corporation. Each division has a P&L, which we run every month. We're very segmented; everybody has to stay in their column because when they don't, you get confusion and squabbles."

"Stay in your column" combined with "maximize your P&L" would seem to be a solid recipe for delegation. After all, if each brother simply maximizes the profit from his part of the business, then wouldn't this result in maximizing the profit of the whole? The answer to this question—unfortunately for managers everywhere—is no. Paul asked about one area where across-column spillovers were likely: "If you're the retail division, one of your most important vendors is the production greenhouse, right? So both P&Ls are going to depend on the price greenhouse charges to retail for petunias. How do you pick that transfer price?"

Getting this price "right" is important, and a quick numerical example (sorry!) will help make the point. Suppose retail is trying to decide how many yellow chrysanthemums to order in a given week. If it orders 30, it's likely that it will sell each for $10. Ordering 50 increases the overall supply and means that retail will only be able to sell each for $8. Suppose further that the cost of growing a yellow mum is $4.

So what's the best price for greenhouse to charge retail? The answer depends on whether we're trying to maximize retail profit, greenhouse profit, or the Berns's overall profit. A transfer price of $4—greenhouse's cost—means that retail will buy 50 mums and earn profit of $4 on each. This yields a total profit of $200. Since greenhouse is pricing at cost, however, it will earn profits of zero.

If, on the other hand, we let greenhouse choose the transfer price, it will prefer something higher. Notice, however, that a higher transfer price will cut into retail's margins; to boost margins and profitability, retail may well reduce the size of its order. If greenhouse sets a transfer price of $6, then an order of 50 mums would result in $2 of margin for retail, and just $100 in retail profit. Greenhouse, in this case, would earn profit of $100. An order of 30 mums, however, would result in $4 of retail margin, $120 in retail profit, and $60 in greenhouse profit.

Note that the greenhouse price—and retail's response to it—will drive the garden center's *overall* profitability. At a transfer price of $4, retail buys 50 mums and the company earns $200. At a transfer price of $6, retail buys 30 mums and overall profits fall to $180. Greenhouse reduces the overall size of the pie by pushing for a bigger slice.

In this example, maximizing greenhouse profit is simply inconsistent with maximizing the company's overall profit. To use a bit of economics jargon, this is because of an "externality" associated with greenhouse's price increase. As greenhouse raises the transfer price beyond cost, retail's profit falls by more than the amount that greenhouse's profit increases. But if the greenhouse manager cares only about his profit, he'll tend to ignore the effect on retail—the effect on retail is "external" to his own P&L, hence the jargon—and we end up with an outcome that maximizes greenhouse profit but not the profit of the entire company.

Such externalities—or cross-column effects—are present any time a manager splits up a business's overall profit into distinct P&Ls that are then used for delegation and performance evaluation. At Midwest Block & Brick, the company's geographic dispersion leads to potential externalities any time salespeople from different regions compete for the same job. If a Union City salesman halves his normal margin to win business that otherwise would have been served by the Paducah plant at the normal margin, then Union City profit rises, but the overall profit falls.

Profit centers and delegation will fail to achieve overall-profit maximization whenever externalities are present, and as a result, these are decisions where top management needs to stay involved. Effective managers learn to spot potential externalities in their organizations and step in to guide local managers to the right choices.

We listened to both Pat Dubbert and Mike Berns talk about how they do this.

"What counts in the big picture," Mike B. said, "is the whole corporate bottom line, whether we shift it to one division or another." But in order to maximize the whole corporate, he's got to put limits in place when externalities are present. He doesn't allow greenhouse to unilaterally set transfer prices; instead, he uses either market-based prices—the wholesale price set by outside greenhouses—or in some cases mandates that the retail buyer work directly with greenhouse to determine production quantities and then insists that the two divisions split the resulting profit. Mike B. uses similar techniques when his landscape division purchases from retail, mostly requiring retail to sell internally at wholesale prices.

Pat Dubbert described the case of a school being built in Columbia, Missouri. Local government projects, he said, often attract bidding contractors from a wide geographic area. His Columbia salespeople might be working with a Columbia contractor on a bid while the Saint Louis salesman works with a competing Saint Louis–based contractor. Pat stays involved to make sure the two work together to avoid giving away margins as they work to help their customer compete.

Richland, Washington
ELEVATE

Identify Interdependent Actions and Coordinate

"It should be here," Paul said.

Gazing through the windshield, Scott and Mike saw a medium-sized strip mall planted on the crest of a hill in Richland, the smallest of the Tri-Cities.

"I see a Baskin-Robbins. And a nail salon," Mike said pointedly.

"It should be here," Paul insisted.

"I knew that adding the which-Tri-City-are-we-in layer of complexity would blow your mind," Scott chided.

Checking his phone again, Paul began to sweat. "Maybe we should have scheduled the uni-city of Walla Walla," Mike quipped, referring to the 30,000-person sweet-onion capital of the world, an hour east.

Paul pointed excitedly. "Oh look," he said, with obvious relief at perhaps not having screwed up after all. "The parking lot winds down in the back."

Scott drove around back where we came upon a lower level—a strip-mall walkout basement of sorts. There, below the Baskin-Robbins, sat the office of Elevate, and we were met at the door by the owner, Paul Carlisle. With sparkling blue eyes, carefully combed but longish hair, and a neat goatee, Paul C. could have been the bass player in a Pearl Jam tribute band if you replaced his white oxford with flannel.

Elevate's business, Paul C. explained, is IT outsourcing for small businesses. "It's very difficult to manage IT people when you're not an IT person," said Paul C., a thoughtful and articulate guy who earned an MBA at Washington State's Tri-Cities campus. "For a small business—where the budget is maybe half a person or one person doing IT—there's really no way to make it work. I put this business together because this task needs to be outsourced.

"Our business is hardware maintenance and end-user support associated with operating systems, servers, and workstations. We also do network infrastructure, but we're not in the business of developing code or programming products. We're currently ten people—me, eight technical people, and one admin."

Elevate exists because of scale economies in hardware maintenance and support. The average cost of maintaining a PC falls as a tech manages more of them, in part because the fixed cost associated with attending training sessions on, for example a new Windows operating system, can be spread out over more machines. Small businesses with relatively few machines can benefit from outsourcing to a specialist who can realize these scale economies.

And this, Paul C. says, means that sometimes clients outgrow him. "We've worked with some fast-growth clients, and if they get to a point where they are using as many resources as a two- or three-person IT department, we'll work with them to transition to an in-house group."

"How do you price this service?" Mike asked.

"We write something like an insurance policy—think of this as managed care for your desktops—and we've got an algorithm that allows us to project what our cost of maintaining your systems is. We use two-year contracts and bill memberships monthly, and then we track which clients are above and below on projected usage. When clients are below, we try to figure out ways to add more value so we can get the renewal. On the flip side, when clients are continually using us more than we expect, we go to them with some consulting recommendations on how to redesign their systems to be more efficient."

"So you're pricing out based on your expectations of your costs," Scott noted. "Why not just bill hourly based on actual?"

Paul C. nodded, having clearly thought hard about this question. "If we bill hourly, then the client is still in a position of having to manage those hours; figure out whether the time is being well spent. The whole point is to get them out of the business of managing IT, which they have zero knowledge about and no interest in doing."

Elevate's main competition comes from insiders—that is, an underscaled internal IT group—and individuals who are "running around pulling stuff out of their trunk; we call them 'trunkers.' And if you're competing against insiders and trunkers, you have to look like a solid firm, the go-to firm when you're finally sick of it. We're super active in the community; I have a hit list of local businesses who should be working with us, and I stay on them. There's a blog I read that talks about the difference between focused sales and stalking, and it's a fine line."

Paul C. is eager to grow, but, like many small business owners, he finds that the big bottleneck is his own time. "The big lump in my gut showed up about a year ago," he said. "That was when the business got big enough that I was swamped. Since then I've been peeling off as much as I can."

While he's been able to farm out some tasks—he says he's shed big chunks of the marketing and accounting, and he's never gotten involved in the day-to-day technical work—he's still directly involved in sales and in the process of devising a long-term service plan for each customer. "The difficulty with my business model from a scalability standpoint has little to do with the technical work and everything to do with the consulting and the needs assessment," he said

"Why can't you hire for the needs assessment?" Scott asked.

Paul C. explained that it's less about finding the right person and more about getting that person to coordinate with the technical side of the business. "There are big cash-flow issues when we bring on new customers," he explained. "It might cost us ten thousand dollars to get your systems up to speed when we come in, and then we're hoping to break even over the two-year contract. Then, on the next contract, we've hopefully built a strong relationship, and we can make some money."

"I don't follow," Scott interrupted. "Where's your cash-flow hit coming from?"

"If I bring on 8 percent additional business this month in onboarding, I can run that on my existing tech capacity. But there was one month where I brought on 22 percent. I had to hire two techs immediately, and that really blew me out of the water. Plus when you're going out to your new client, you're visiting the existing client less."

"Oh, I see," Mike said. "Successful selling means investing in more employees, but your payback period on that investment is maybe twenty-four to thirty-six months."

"Right," said Paul C. "I can't bring too many new customers on at once. And what salesperson wants to hear that?"

Paul Carlisle's problem is one of coordinating the actions of his employees. To get sales and consulting off his desk, he'd ideally like to hire a commission-based salesperson/consultant and turn that individual loose to stalk, er, call on the small business owners of the Tri-Cities. Such an incentive plan would motivate high sales effort and likely generate lots of new customers. But unfortunately, this isn't what Paul C. needs. Here, the value of a new customer, and hence the value of a salesperson's effort, depends very much on whether the technical side of the business has excess capacity. Paul C. doesn't want high sales effort all the time; he wants high sales effort when there's excess tech capacity, but low sales effort when the techs are swamped. Delegation with commissions won't achieve this form of coordination, and Paul C. will need to stay actively involved.

The key to spotting a potential coordination problem is to look for interdependence of the "right" employee actions. If you need one employee to zig when another zags, that's a case where coordination is important. How are such problems different from externalities? With externalities, the actions of one part of the organization affect the *profits* of another part; recall that if Mike Berns's greenhouse charges a high price to retail for purple petunias, the profit of greenhouse rises, but the profit of retail falls by more. With coordination, the actions of one part affect the *right action* of another part: Elevate needs a salesperson who will vary his or her effort in accordance with the demands on the tech side of the business.

The standard recipe for delegation—cut the organization into pieces taking account of who is likely to be able to access relevant information, measure the contribution of each piece to profits, and delegate decision-making—can fail when the divisions need to coordinate their actions. Effective managers need to be able to spot situations where divisions need to coordinate and step in to guide local managers to the right outcomes. As Paul C. peels off work to hand to subordinates, he'll need to remain involved in consulting and needs assessment to make sure this task stays in sync with his technical staff.

As we drove away from Elevate, Scott began comparing Paul Carlisle's coordination problems to those he was encountering at the School of Business. "We have this issue with course scheduling. Our undergraduate advising department is communicating with students about when courses are offered, but department chairs are setting class times. The problem is that…"

"Wait a second," Paul interrupted, clearly irked with Scott for oversharing. "It's great that you've diagnosed this coordination problem. Are you able to actually do anything about it?"

"Well, um…"

"Those who can't do…" Mike quipped. "Have you considered going back to teaching?"

Mazzeo's Law

Delegating Decisions: What It Depends On

- **Information:** At Midwest Products Group, local plant managers are in the best position to gather information about production bottlenecks and inventory, and it makes sense to delegate operational decisions to them as a result.

- **Incentives:** By tying plant-manager pay to plant-level profits, Midwest Products provides good incentives for operational decisions. CEO Pat Dubbert keeps HR decisions on his desk, however, concerned that the profit-based incentives won't be sufficient to motivate plant managers to distinguish between good and bad performers.

- **Performance Measures:** Short-run accounting profits and long-term value aren't always the same thing, as Silverwood Theme Park found when food and beverage managers skimped on quality to improve short-term numbers. Delegation strategies work best when managers identify performance measures that correspond well with long-term value.

- **Externalities:** An externality results when one division's pursuit of profit adversely affects the profitability of other divisions. At Berns Garden Center, the production greenhouse could boost its profit by raising the prices it charges to retail, but doing so would reduce the company's overall profit. Delegating the pricing decision to the greenhouse would lead to problems.

- **Coordination:** When there are interdependencies between the right actions, delegation with strong incentives for divisional performance can lead to coordination problems. At Elevate, Paul Carlisle worried that a commissioned sales team would chase customers too aggressively and overwhelm his technical teams.

CHAPTER 10

Battling the Big Boys

"So when are you guys going to actually *write* this book?"

Each of us had been hearing this refrain from friends, colleagues, and students with increasing frequency. For some time, we had been describing the lessons from our travels to fellow professors at academic conferences and using stories from the road to illustrate key points in class. But after a couple of years, we began to worry that our colleagues and students would think we were only in it for the road trips.

To get us going, Mike posted audio files from our interviews on a shared Dropbox folder, while Paul contributed photos and video. Scott, who had saved a stack of napkins containing our dinnertime notes, meticulously scanned them into his computer, scraping off bits of barbeque sauce on occasion. The actual writing came in fits and starts as we worked independently at our respective universities. But occasionally we got together in person to hash out ideas and to brainstorm on themes and format.

We chose the mountains of Northern California for the last of these powwows; the area is Paul's wintertime ski destination, and he knew of nice houses for rent in the summer at off-season rates (much appreciated by price-sensitive Scott). While we were enjoying the Sierras and discussing the various chapters, we came to a somewhat troubling realization.

"We are writing a book about small business, and we never visited an independent bookstore!"

A few phone calls later, we had a meeting with Christine Kelly, owner of Sundance Books and Music in Reno, Nevada. The next day we made the hour-long drive from our rental house in Truckee.

"Can we stop at Circus Circus afterward?" Mike piped up from the backseat, recalling unfinished blackjack business from the casinos of Council Bluffs.

Unfortunately, Scott needed to get to the airport right after our meeting—he mumbled something about a date that night back home—so we bypassed the ostentation and glitz of the "Biggest Little City in the World." A mile south, on the other side of the Truckee River, we came upon a large classically styled house with a well-tended lawn and flowering bushes in the front. "Sundance Books and Music" was wedged in small lettering on the beam above the columns.

Reno, Nevada
SUNDANCE BOOKS AND MUSIC

Focus on What the Big Boys Don't Do Well

We walked in and looked around a bit before meeting Christine. The house, which we later learned was built in 1906 and measures over 5,000 square feet, was divided into several small rooms on multiple floors in which books were displayed in cases against walls and on tables in the center. Chairs and benches were scattered throughout. It was quiet in the store just after lunchtime on a Friday, with a few customers milling about and one employee at a register in front. We meandered, browsing the eclectic selection as we waited.

After a quick greeting, Christine led us up a couple of flights of stairs to her office in the house's attic. A tall woman in her forties with long, straight brown hair, Christine exuded a laid-back personality and would have fit better in hippie-town Missoula than in gaudy Reno. A large desk took up much of the space, with a bookcase behind containing autographed copies left over from book-signing events. A few old displays, including a large cutout illustration of that Wimpy Kid with the Diary, crowded the back corner of the room.

As we had expected, Christine described a very competitive bookselling landscape. When the business started in 1985, she said, being an independent bookstore was what she called a "great market space." But, over time, things got considerably more difficult. "Even before the Internet got solid," she recalled, "what we started to see in the nineties was the advent of the megastore like Barnes and Noble and Borders. At about the same time, we also saw the emergence of stores like Costco. And the result was the erosion of a certain kind of book selling for us. Predominantly, they sold *New York Times* Best Seller list books at a heavy discount—30 percent off."

Naturally, we asked Christine whether she tried to discount the best sellers as well in an effort to keep those sales at Sundance and out of Borders and Costco and Amazon. She said

she didn't. In fact, she greatly reduced her inventory in this category despite the fact that best sellers had previously been a
good market for her.

"I refuse to do that," Christine said, "because there's no way
that I can play that ballgame. And you look like you're trying to
keep up with the neighbor. There's no way you can compete."

Paul asked the question that we were all thinking: "So, how
do you make it these days?"

"I have no idea," she joked.

Christine proceeded to explain how her intuition and experience have guided her strategy in recent years. She does
a variety of things to clearly distinguish Sundance from the
larger price-discounting competitors. She expends considerable effort "curating" her shelves, making sure that there is
a diverse collection of books available to her customers, who
often browse for thirty minutes or more before making a purchase. She works to retain key staff, whom customers look to
for recommendations and a familiar face. She organizes events
that resonate with the local audience. Christine even started a
small publishing arm that focuses on regional authors (such as
cartoonist Brian Crane from nearby Sparks) and stories (a biog-
raphy of LaVere Redfield, an eccentric billionaire from Reno,
is in the works).

And that's how she "makes it these days," to answer Paul's
question. The number of independent bookstores in the
United States has dropped by more than half over the past
twenty years as competition has taken its toll. That Sundance
still remains is a testament to Christine's effective, if humble,
approach.

The lineup of large competitors faced by Sundance is emblematic of the challenges facing many small businesses today. Large companies—the "Big Boys," as we call them—do a number of things extremely well and can be tough competitors. There are, however, many activities that *small* businesses are uniquely well suited to perform, as well as important tasks that big companies struggle with. Successfully competing with the Big Boys requires a solid understanding of the advantages *and disadvantages* of scale. As Mazzeo's Law would suggest, the right strategy will often depend on how these plusses and minuses apply in a specific situation.

Pueblo, Colorado
GPS SOURCE

Avoid Silos by Over-Sharing

It was a wintry January day when we visited Pueblo, Colorado. Anticipating weather trouble, we orchestrated a switch from our assigned rental sedan to a four-wheel-drive SUV at the Denver airport. Scott's time in Utah came in handy, as he was able to navigate the snowy one-hundred-mile drive to Pueblo with relative ease.

Relieved to have arrived safely, we headed off to visit GPS Source, an engineering company located just off US 50 west of town. The business is housed in a nondescript warehouse and shares a parking lot with a repair shop guarded by a scary-looking dog. We charmed our way past Cujo and met with Allen Gross, the founder and president of the company. Allen looked the part of an engineer-turned-businessman, sporting a thick beard but also neatly attired in a fresh polo shirt. We took seats in front of Allen's cluttered desk, facing bookshelves crowded with work binders and pictures of teenaged children. An official photo of President George W. Bush completed the scene.

"GPS is inherently a weak signal coming from the satellites," Allen explained to us. "So if you're outside, you can get GPS just fine, but if you come indoors, it doesn't get through the walls or through the ceiling. We bring GPS from outdoors to indoors—the antennas and cables and splitters and amplifiers. We take the signal, make it stronger, and then distribute it inside buildings."

Paul took the leap and asked the really naïve question that we all had in mind: "Why do you need GPS indoors?"

"Test," Allen replied, "A lot of manufacturers that build GPS would have to go outside to test the equipment. If they want to test anything live, they have to bring the signal inside."

As the testing requirements become more complex, customers want more capabilities with the signal once it is brought inside. GPS Source has developed and sold technologies for these applications. "We've branched into developing smarter products; we now have computer processing inside the systems that allows us to do digital control to vary the strength of the signal via Bluetooth, for example."

We wondered how a relatively small firm like GPS Source, with just a couple dozen employees and less than $5 million per year in revenue, could compete in an engineering-intensive field such as this. Large competitors with more engineers, bigger budgets, and global reach would seem to have many advantages. In talking with Allen, it became clear that figuring out how to direct their engineers' efforts efficiently was critical to their business. If they had a good idea about exactly what problems to solve, it would matter less that they had fewer resources at their disposal to solve them.

"We listen. The customers usually tell you what to do," Allen said. "They are always talking about what they wish they could do. You have to listen, collect that data, and develop products to answer some of those questions."

Allen described a recent example. "One of the larger contracts that we won recently was building a re-transmission system inside C-17 military aircraft. Their payloads now have GPS and when they push them out the back of a C-17—unless there was GPS inside the aircraft—it took them a few minutes to acquire the signal. So we now transmit GPS in the back of C-17s so that payload is live. Basically, it thinks it has GPS— which it does—and so when it rolls out the door, it's seamless. It's tracking immediately."

Winning this military contract required competing against much larger companies; giants like Northrop Grumman and Lockheed Martin have substantially more experience in bidding for this type of work. However, GPS Source was at an advantage in this case because they had more knowledge about what the customer needed.

"The technology that we used to do the C-17 contract—we had heard about the need from customers. The first version we built was a piece of crap, but what we learned by doing that gave us the knowledge we needed to do the C-17 contract. We knew more than anyone else in the world because we had already built the product."

Based on information from customers, GPS Source had identified a problem that needed to be solved. The engineers developed technology, and then the military wrote specifications in the request for proposals that matched what GPS Source had developed. It became a contract that GPS Source could win against just about anyone.

Phil Coiner, the firm's chief technology officer, sneaked into the office behind us as we were listening to Allen talk. Phil credited Allen with making the connection between the market need and the firm's technical capabilities. Pointing at Allen, Phil said, "It's because he answered the phone when the customer called. You really don't have to think of anything in this business—your customer will call you up and tell you what the next thing ought to be."

As the company got a bit larger, Allen was not always able to answer the phone; most customer interaction has shifted to dedicated salespeople. But GPS Source is still small enough that the message can get from the customers to the engineers efficiently. There is only one water cooler at GPS Source—the sales guys and the engineers can't *avoid* talking to each other.

Allen summarized the issue. "We discuss that all the time. The salespeople can come back with a handful of cards, but if they can't give you information about what's going on in the market, you won't know what to do next."

Why can't larger companies share information between sales and engineering as well as GPS Source can? The reasons have to do largely with the challenges of effective delegation we discussed in chapter 9. Large firms must, almost by definition given their scale, rely on delegation. But effective delegation requires partitioning of responsibilities paired with strong incentives tied to narrow performance measures. A sales division in a large organization, for example, would typically face performance targets tied to sales (not overall profits). This narrow measure, however, means that salespeople have little reason to think about how to help engineering.

Large organizations have a strong tendency to develop silos, with employees working in isolation instead of in tandem and ignoring externalities. It is common for the marketing and engineering divisions to end up in intense battles as each focuses too much on its own issues: Engineers accuse marketing of selling things they can't build, while marketing gripes that the engineers don't build anything they can sell.

This bias toward siloing in large organizations isn't the result of bad management; quite the reverse, in fact. Delegation and narrowing of performance measures are exactly the right choices for large-firm managers to make when trying to manage so many people and activities. And this means weak across-division communication is an almost unavoidable side effect of growth; the Big Boys are just going to be bad at it.

GPS Source can compete better against the Big Boys because its "internal information processing" capability is superior—precisely because the company is not big enough to have multiple silos. The key insight from GPS Source is to recognize the advantage that comes from being small and to exploit the smooth communication capabilities in choosing activities. GPS Source will never have an R&D budget the size of one of their big aerospace competitors. But, by listening to customers and doing smart R&D, they can win some contracts. Even as the little guy.

Spartanburg, South Carolina
LAUNCH SOMETHING

Provide Services That Don't Require Large Overhead Investments

"Did you know the Marshall Tucker Band is from Spartanburg?" Paul asked, researching the town via smartphone from the passenger seat.

"That's awesome," Scott said, launching into a few horribly sung bars of the band's 1973 hit "Can't You See."

Mike cringed as Paul nodded along. "That song is the second best use of a flute in classic rock," Paul opined.

"Well, how can you top Jethro Tull?" Scott agreed. "You'll never see another rock flautist."

Spartanburg, which boasts a population of 37,000, has a long history in textile manufacturing, but the downtown area was hit hard by the recent recession and financial crisis. The economic outlook seemed brighter when we arrived at the offices of Launch Something for our 8:30 meeting with the company's founder, Sims Bouwmeester. We parked in a small lot behind a large well-kept house just east of downtown and were greeted by Sims, a woman in her early thirties with long brown hair and a bright-blue sweater.

Launch Something does marketing strategy consulting for local businesses and organizations in the Spartanburg area. It is a relatively new company—not quite six years old at the time of our visit—and as we learned, it had been busy almost right from the start. When we asked Sims what sorts of services the company offered, the list was quite substantial.

"We do marketing," Sims began, "branding, name creation, logo design. Positioning the brand through collaterals—printed materials, brochures, product catalogs, anything that's printed or produced."

"Advertising," she continued, "from print, online, outdoor, broadcast TV and radio. And then, of course, strategy, which is the thing that got us a lot of our clients in the beginning. Help figure out how they are going to get from point A to point B through marketing, and earn more profits."

Sims said she has seven full-time employees—and had had as many as ten, pre-recession—but has learned to fill in the gaps with talented freelancers. "People are constantly sending résumés to us, but I grapple with the question of 'Do I hire full-time or do I just cultivate some really great outsource relationships?' If we have a specific job, whether it's a web developer or if we need help with a PR project, we do a short-term freelance."

We were very curious about how a company offering this collection of services would get its start and how its own "launch" would go. "I'm from Spartanburg, but then went away for school," Sims explained, describing studies in New Hampshire and Scotland. Working for an ad agency in New York, she found she "really enjoyed bringing business structure to the creative process, even though I wasn't the one doing the creative work."

After picking up a pair of graduate degrees, Sims came home to start her business, relying at first on a network of family connections. "It's a small town, and people knew me. My family is here; my cousin owns the oldest bar in Spartanburg, half a block down. We threw a little bit of an opening party, marketed ourselves with the website, and got local media coverage."

While connections might get you a meeting, they won't get you a customer unless you also offer a compelling value proposition; that is, something you offer that's over and above what the competition can do. Sims described several Big Boy advertising agencies in the Spartanburg area that operated in a traditional manner. These larger companies were built around scale economies of the type we described in chapter 1. They had made substantial fixed investments in managerial overhead necessary to provide a one-stop marketing shop for clients who have a substantial need for strategic marketing services. To offset these fixed costs, large agencies typically require their customers to sign an expensive, multiyear retainer agreement to do the work.

Launch Something offered an attractive alternative. "We've always been 'project-based,'" Sims said. "We initially attracted a whole swarm of midlevel companies where they couldn't afford a retainer that was five to ten thousand dollars a month, where they were guaranteeing it for a year to three years. But they could do a three-month project that was ten thousand.

"That quickly got us a lot of referrals, and in our first year, we had almost a hundred different clients," she said. "We started with mostly small retail businesses, but it's slowly started to shift to larger organizations."

"Can you give us an example of project-based work you've done for a larger client?" Mike asked.

Sims nodded and described her relationship with the national restaurant chain Denny's, which is headquartered in Spartanburg. "They have a very large contract with a national ad agency; they're doing Super Bowl ads and national campaigns. But that contract doesn't include their internal marketing. Suppose they have a new product; they have to figure out how they're going to market that to their own employees. They have incentive programs and do a lot of training here in Spartanburg. For something like that, they'd end up way overpaying for something with their agency," Sims remarked. "Fifteen thousand dollars for a brochure that should cost six hundred." Denny's reaped some real savings by working with Launch Something instead.

Sims Bouwmeester followed a winning recipe for competing with the Big Boys—provide something consumers value that the Big Boys can't provide. In this case, consumers wanted high-quality marketing consulting services on small projects. While the large advertising agencies weren't set up to do small projects at a reasonable price because of their overhead, Launch Something focused on just those types of projects. While the individual projects are relatively small, the number of interested clients is substantial. Not bad in an economic environment where it's very hard to get a business started and where even the Big Boys are struggling.

Bloomington, Illinois
PRENZLER OUTDOOR ADVERTISING

Exploit Local Information to Differentiate Your Product

On a drizzly mid-April day in Bloomington, Illinois, we visited the office of Prenzler Outdoor Advertising. Erik Prenzler, a tall man in his mid-fifties with a mop of wavy light-brown hair, owns the business and welcomed us in from the rain. Erik looked tired at our 8:00 a.m. meeting and was clearly a bit cranky.

"I pay a lot of taxes," Erik groused before we even really got started with our interview, "and last night, my accountant told me how much I owe."

"It just put me in a good mood," he said sarcastically.

Honestly, we weren't in the best mood either. Big thunderstorms had hit Chicago the previous night, and flight delays led to a late departure on our drive to Bloomington. Paul had been traveling with his son, David, who was continuing on to the East Coast to visit Brown University, where he had just been admitted. Because of the storms, David missed his connection and would be arriving in Boston too late to catch the bus to Providence. To make matters worse, David had recently broken his ankle playing baseball, so he was traveling in a cast and walking on crutches.

So as we made our way south from O'Hare, Paul scrolled through his contacts list, calling colleagues, friends, and acquaintances—really anyone who might be able to pick David up after midnight at the Boston airport and let him sleep on a couch. The best call we overheard was to an ex-girlfriend, who must have been really surprised to hear this message on her voicemail: "Hi, this is Paul Oyer. I know you haven't heard from me in a while, and I have kind of an odd request…"

To make matters worse, a torrential rain pelted us on the entire drive to Bloomington. It was too late to find anything decent to eat, so we settled for fast food at a highway exit. We couldn't even agree on what to eat—Scott dropped Mike

and Paul off (not very close to the entrance) at McDonald's
and went to a different joint across the street. The short night's
sleep didn't improve our attitudes much.

"We picked the wrong week to be traveling," Mike commented. "Tax day will wreck everyone's mood."

Erik proceeded to explain the outdoor-advertising business —
his company owns easements and has leases on properties where
they erect billboards. Erik then sells advertising on these billboards to companies that want to reach local consumers. He
started twenty years earlier with a single billboard and has added
three or four each year since. At the time of our visit, Erik was up
to sixty billboards, and he was scouting locations to add a couple
more.

"Today I'm hoping to get a ten-year lease from a guy on
Main Street. I've been working with him for forty-five days. I
want to put up an LED there."

Along with obtaining the billboards and selling the advertising, Prenzler is also responsible for maintaining the advertising
on the billboard while the company is providing the space.
This can end up being a lot of tedious work, as Erik described.
"The biggest thing about billboards, man, is that they are up
all the time. One hundred percent of my boards are lighted. I
am the guy that looks at them and, if the light bulbs are out,
they're gonna get changed."

"I drive around at night and look at lights," Erik elaborated,
which sounded a lot more soulful than what economists typically do at night.

As we continued to talk about Erik's business, the conversation turned to the competition. Like many other media industries, billboard advertising has seen considerable

consolidation—with large companies accumulating substantial networks of billboards. These Big Boys have scale advantages in things like purchasing and billing, can serve large customers needing exposure in many locations efficiently, and can often bundle their billboards along with advertising opportunities in other media that they also hold. They use these advantages to keep their prices low.

"My biggest competitor out here is Lamar," Erik explained. "They're a publicly traded company out of Baton Rouge." Indeed, Lamar is a huge company compared to Erik's, boasting nearly 150,000 displays and selling advertising through over 200 regional offices. Two other Big Boys in the industry—CBS Outdoor and Clear Channel—own a wide variety of media types, including radio and television stations along with over a million billboards and other outdoor-advertising locations between them.

How does Erik manage to survive as the little guy in competition with powerful competitors undercutting on price? As we discussed in chapter 3, product differentiation can help firms avoid tough price competition. Indeed, Erik insisted that he was able to maintain revenue because he offered customers higher "quality." We were initially skeptical—what is a "high-quality" billboard, exactly?

Erik volunteered two possibilities: "I just feel that I have better locations. And I offer better service."

On locations, information is critical. Subtle factors affect a billboard's effectiveness—a board located near a longer stoplight, for example, will expose drivers to the advertising message longer. By virtue of his experience and his deep knowledge of the area, Erik can make better decisions about where to place billboards. Customers find Erik's billboards more attractive because advertising on them reaches more potential customers.

Erik is also able to obtain better locations because of his engagement with the community. We asked Erik why the Big Boys can't outbid him for the best billboard spots—for example, that attractive location on Main Street that Erik is trying to acquire for a new LED.

"They don't even know about it," he says of the competition. "I know more people—it helps."

Local information also allows Erik to respond more quickly to customers' requests. He can maintain his boards better and provide a higher-quality product to his customers. "One customer—they do a ton of billboards. They're a chain restaurant company, their agency is based out of Nashville. They'll drive by and send me an email and they'll say, 'There's a wrinkle' or they'll say, 'Hey, look, one of our guys went by the board and there are two lights out.'"

It's not surprising that such a customer would appreciate and demand that their billboards be well maintained. As Erik related to us, billboard advertising is their bread and butter.

"As far as I know, they use exclusively billboards. They don't use any other type of advertising. So for one store they might have three or four billboards. And that's a good amount of money—because their customers, it's all travelers. I keep the lights on. I keep the wrinkles off the boards. They give you forty-eight hours—and then they want you to take a picture and prove it to them," Erik recounted.

The Big Boys, Erik said, aren't set up to provide that level of quality. "They have a lot of inventory to manage. They're in Decatur; they're in Bloomington. I think they have some boards in Springfield. They manage them all out of Decatur. They do not have an office here in town."

Prenzler Outdoor Advertising may have to work hard to maintain these advantages. While LED technology brings many benefits to the outdoor advertising market, it requires less maintenance—in terms of burned-out bulbs and wrinkled edges—than traditional vinyl and paper. This technological change could erode one source of advantage for the little guy, and Erik may need to search for other ways to exploit local information to stay ahead.

Columbus, Indiana
HOOSIER SPORTING GOODS

Invest in Effort-Intensive Activities if the Big Boys Have Incentive Problems

As we left Bloomington, Paul's son called, having arrived safely at Brown after spending the night on the Cambridge, Massachusetts, couch of a former colleague. Paul's ex-girlfriend rang soon after, and the two had a pleasant fifteen-minute chat as we crossed the state line into Indiana.

Rolling past Indianapolis on the interstate, we arrived in Columbus, Indiana, where we couldn't help but notice that things in town were a little different. Most of the places we visited had been more like Spartanburg, with little traffic and empty storefronts on "Main Street."

The heart of Columbus, however, appeared quite healthy,

with many open businesses on the almost bustling main drag. Washington (not Main) Street is a wide boulevard with diagonal parking, and a line of tall leafy trees separating the cars from the sidewalk. According to locals, mayors in Columbus have been encouraging and promoting the downtown for at least three decades. Columbus is also fortunate to be the headquarters location of Cummins Inc., a Fortune 500 company that manufactures engines and had made a major commitment to downtown. Just off Washington Street, construction was under way on a large facility to include residential units and parking for headquarters' employees. It was the only time during our trips that we saw a construction crane in the old part of any town.

At 611 Washington Street, we met Mike Bodart, owner of Hoosier Sporting Goods, and joined him at a table that was made out of a glass basketball backboard. Hoosier is something of an institution in Columbus—at least seventy years old—and although just in his mid-thirties, Mike has already had a long history with the company. He shopped there as a child and, as he explained, took an interest in the business from a very early age.

"I'll tell you an inside story," Mike B. related. "When the guy we bought the company from bought the store in 1986, I was eleven years old. My dad came home one day and said, 'Herschel Crippen bought Hoosier Sporting Goods.'"

"I said, 'Well, you can tell him that in about fifteen years, I'll be ready to buy it!'" Mike B. recalled. "I was off by about a year and a half. I always knew that I was eventually going to be here."

"You were an unusual child," Scott noted. Mike B. agreed and didn't take offense.

It was easy to see why a small-town, sports-loving kid would fall in love with Hoosier Sporting Goods. The store was lined with baseball bats and basketballs, with most of the apparel in the colors of the local high schools. Mike B. was holding a baseball glove as we talked and was the picture of the high-school sports star all grown-up.

"Sports have always been a huge part of my life," Mike B. reminisced. "When we played Little League baseball, we would come down to the store and get the uniforms. There was a guy who worked here, who had been here forever, and he was nice and knew our names. He made it a big deal.

"It was just *a lot* of good experiences. You know, it's one of those stores that you walk into that's older—it has a smell. I'll come back from the bank sometimes and I open up the door and 'Aaah.' It's just like thirty years ago."

It was at about this point that the unsentimental voice of the economist had to be brought into the conversation. Paul spoiled the mood by bluntly turning from smells and memories to the bottom line.

"OK, so you've bought this place—now you've got to make a living out of running it. So how's that been going?"

Hoosier Sporting Goods has some things on its side. Mike B. is a smart, enthusiastic owner, and the continued economic activity in Columbus (even through the financial crisis and recession) certainly didn't hurt. And kids are always going to need baseball gloves and basketballs.

But, as is true in the book-selling business, big-box stores have come to dominate sporting goods over the last few decades. With scale comes buying clout and cheaper regional and national advertising; a big chain like Dick's Sporting

Goods could almost certainly squeeze a lower price out of Prenzler Outdoor Advertising than Hoosier Sporting Goods could. And this means lower costs and, potentially, lower prices for customers. Indeed, Hoosier Sporting Goods had competition from national chains MC Sports and Hibbett Sports, both of which had mall-based outlets in Columbus.

Mike B. talked about how he was able to remain viable in the midst of the Big Boys in his market.

"We have extremely loyal customers," he started out, "because of how we treat them. I had a customer who complained to me after going to one of my competitors, 'They couldn't tell me anything! I said, screw them—I'm coming to Hoosiers.'"

"We follow up with our customers. I'll tell most of our customers, 'You can always find this cheaper. If you want to search high and low—you're probably going to find it cheaper. But, if you have a problem with it, you don't have anyone to call. If you have a problem with this, we will solve it.'"

This strategy will only work if the product being sold is somehow complicated or unusual so that Hoosier's superior knowledge is valuable to customers. Otherwise, there would be few problems to solve, and buying decisions would be more focused on price.

Acknowledging this, Mike B. adjusts his inventory to accentuate his advantage. "I refuse to carry something that they can walk into Walmart or Target and buy."

Other merchandising decisions take advantage of Mike's local knowledge and effort spent on making connections with the community.

"We've been in it long enough to know when the football season starts—when the little kids start buying their football stuff. We have our stuff, and it's ready to go. For our big competitor, every year I open up the Sunday paper to their ad and I laugh. Five weeks after football starts, they're advertising their football equipment."

As another example, Mike B. cited the local football rivalry. "When the two high schools—East and North—play each other in football each year, it's just nuts. The whole week is nuts. One high school is blue and white, the other is brown and orange—those are the school colors. There's a line out the door to make custom T-shirts." Unless you were in tune with the local community, you wouldn't stock a lot of brown-and-orange T-shirts.

Hoosier also tries to convert its connections in the local area to sales for the store. Mike B. told us about employees who take orders from the field while playing in local softball leagues. Customers call him at home on weekend nights to place special orders. Being involved in the sports community in Columbus is an important part of that customer engagement. "I try to stay in contact with the right coaches at the high school level."

Mike B. is, in effect, a walking billboard for the store. "People see me and they associate me with the store," he explained. "I was walking down to the bank the other day. A guy walks out of the bank on the way to his car and says, 'Hey there—I need to go down to your store.' And he gets out of his car and walks down to the store."

"If I'm out running errands or something like that, I'm wearing a Hoosier Sporting Goods T-shirt. Sometimes I get tired of wearing them, but that's permanent advertising."

As we discussed in chapter 8, it is often difficult to provide employees with the right incentives to put in the effort to move the company ahead. The managers of local chain sporting-goods stores are likely to have different interests from those of the company owners, and aligning these interests through pay-for-performance can be tricky.

To see why, note that many of Mike B.'s activities center on building relationships in the community. He gets to know the local coaches, the local high schools, and the local schedules, and these activities represent a long-term investment. Mike is not trying to boost short-run sales to hit a current profit target; instead, he's trying to build the long-run value of his business.

The owner of a Big Boy chain might want a store manager to make similar long-term investments in the community, but finding the right performance measure to motivate this activity is hard. Accounting profit, as we saw in chapter 9, is inherently a short-run number, and it can be difficult to get an employee to think about long-run value.

And because it's hard to incorporate long-term value into a performance measure, the Big Boys are unlikely to be very good at activities where the payoffs are long-term. It's another unavoidable side effect of growth. This provides a wonderful opportunity for owner/managers like Mike B., where incentive problems are moot.

But just as with Leah McMahon's coffee shop, there are limits to the potential for Mike Bodart to expand his business. It would be difficult for him to be so active in more than one community at the same time. If he opened in another town or two, he would quickly be spread too thin to become friendly with all the local coaches. Hiring local managers is an option, but he'd likely have the same challenge in motivating them that the big chains do.

As we strolled down Washington Street in search of lunch after our visit to Hoosier Sporting Goods, we reminisced about our own childhood sports memories. Mike's game was basketball and Paul's was tennis, but neither had as much success as Scott, who started at quarterback for his high school in the homecoming game his junior year.

"Wow!" said Paul, who hadn't heard that story before. "How'd you do?"

"Threw four interceptions in the first half. Never played again," was the sad reply. Scott, it seems, struggled mightily when competing against the Big Boys.

Mazzeo's Law

Battling the Big Boys: What It Depends On

- **Understanding the Big Boys' Strengths:** It is important for small businesses not to waste effort in activities for which large size helps; competing on the same turf as the Big Boys is not likely to be a winning strategy. Christine Kelly avoided discounting best sellers since she understood that she would never win a pricing game against the chains.
- **Exploiting the Big Boys' Weaknesses:** At GPS Source, the engineers efficiently solve customers' problems brought to

them by salespeople, while delegation challenges make such internal communications difficult in larger companies. The large sporting-goods chains have trouble providing incentives for local store managers to be as motivated as Mike Bodart, giving him an advantage in effort-intensive activities.

- **Offering Services the Big Boys Don't:** Large competitors invest in overhead to exploit their size, enabling them to perform certain activities efficiently. Launch Something focused instead on the smaller advertising and consulting projects that larger agencies weren't set up to do well.
- **Utilizing Smaller Size to Differentiate:** In many cases, these advantages are connected to the efficient acquisition and use of local information. Erik Prenzler uses his knowledge and contacts to identify good locations and respond quickly to service issues, meaning higher-quality billboards for customers.

Strategy Is a Continuous Process

The people of Hattiesburg, Mississippi, have to be hearty and adaptable. Just seventy miles north of the Gulf of Mexico, the town was severely damaged by 130-mile-per-hour winds during Hurricane Katrina, and the storm's effects were still evident during our visit some years later.

Luckily, we did not see anything that severe, though we did manage to get a sampling of the local weather. We arrived on a clear and temperate January evening and enjoyed a not-exactly-low-calorie dinner involving beer and jambalaya at the Crescent City Grill. Waking to sun the next morning, Paul enjoyed a run through the green countryside, but as we hopped into our rental, the beautiful day took a turn for the worse. The sky blackened, and the ten-minute drive to our meeting was a dream come true for any Weather Channel junkie. The winds howled, rain fell in horizontal sheets, and stoplights swayed on the street corners.

"I'm not getting out of the car," Paul said as we arrived. "I'll ruin my one decent pair of shoes."

Ignoring the obvious opening to critique Paul's taste in footwear, Mike turned to Scott. "Who are we meeting with?"

"Megagate," Scott replied.

"Megadeth?" Paul said, mishearing due to the pelting rain on the roof of the car.

Megadeth was a 1980s metal band that sold more than 50 million records. At least a couple of those were to Scott, who, in addition to his almost maniacal obsession with the band Rush, is a regular at concerts of AC/DC and Def Leppard. In more than one Starbucks during our travels, Scott was caught mumbling "pour some sugar on me" as he sweetened his coffee.

"Mega*gate*," Scott repeated with exasperation. "Megadeth is from Southern California, so why would they have an office here?"

We have argued throughout this book that there are no one-size-fits-all answers in business strategy. Effective strategy requires that you understand your markets, understand your employees, understand your organization, and then tailor your strategic choices to the particulars. But like the Hattiesburg weather—or, for that matter, the fashion statements of metal bands—the business environment is one of constant change. Competition arises, regulations are imposed, input prices and wages fluctuate, and technology marches steadily forward. So even if you have a perfect strategy, are executing effectively, and have established a comfortable competitive advantage, you had better be anticipating what the right strategy will be for tomorrow.

So we add a final corollary to Mazzeo's Law:

> **Corollary 3**
> Strategy is never a solved problem.

Because strategy must be tailored to the specifics, and the specific features of the business environment are in constant motion, strategy itself is a moving target.

Hattiesburg, Mississippi
MEGAGATE

Don't Count on Today's Strategy for Tomorrow

Megagate, located west of town on US 98, is a telecommunications company serving the local business community. "Think AT&T, but much, much smaller," said Kevin Pack, the company's CEO. Clean-cut and in his forties, Kevin wore a blue-striped tie over a white shirt and would not have looked out of place behind the anchor's desk at SportsCenter. We guessed he had probably never heard of Megadeth.

Kevin showed us into his spacious office, which featured an impressive view of the receding storm through the large windows. Two football jerseys—Brett Favre's Packers #4 and Steve Young's 49ers #8—hung, autographed, in frames above his desk. Favre is a local hero, having played his college ball at the University of Southern Mississippi in town.

Like all Hattiesburg residents, Kevin and Megagate have

had to be resilient in the face of changing weather. "The roof from the building next door came through this window during Hurricane Katrina, and our building took a half million dollars' damage. The Steve Young jersey was right down there," Kevin said, pointing out the window, "on top of that drain in a bunch of debris. You can see that the signature is a little faded."

But an even bigger challenge has been riding the waves of the ever-changing telecommunications business. The company was born when Kevin's business partner bid for, and won, the initial license to provide cellular service in the Hattiesburg market. Joining forces with the group that won the license for the nearby Laurel market, the company was an early entrant into cellular telephone service. Holding a strong barrier to entry due to the limited number of licenses, Kevin and his partner worked to educate potential customers, price the product according to customer willingness-to-pay, and sign up as many as they profitably could. The cellular market grew faster than expected. Kevin remembered, "When the business started, the ten-year business plan hoped for a couple thousand customers. A few years later, we had sixty thousand."

With the growth came new challenges. Specifically, the barrier to entry was not as long lasting as Megagate might have hoped. "The local cellular market went from a duopoly to more competition," Kevin said. "There was a lot of downward pressure on pricing, and big carriers introduced nationwide plans. We had to follow suit and introduce nationwide plans. The problem was that we had an eleven-county footprint. So any time a customer went outside the eleven-county area, we were paying roaming."

This gradual change in customer preferences toward national plans favored the Big Boys, and economies of scale soon allowed AT&T, Sprint, and others to dominate. Megagate found its assets were worth more when it was part of a larger company than when it operated as an independent little guy. Maximizing value meant selling, and this is precisely what Kevin did. The Megagate cellular business became part of Alltel and was eventually folded into Verizon.

But this was hardly the end for the entrepreneurial minds of Kevin and his team. Megagate had started to offer local and long-distance landline service, and this business was left behind after the sale. "Alltel didn't want it," he said. "It had about a million dollars a year in revenue. It couldn't support the people and the infrastructure on its own, so we built it into something. We started offering dial-up Internet service, and before we knew it, we had thousands of dial-up customers."

The dial-up business was, in some ways, similar to the cellular market. Megagate was selling a new way of accessing telecommunication services, which meant that educating potential customers was a key success factor. But as with the cellular market, Megagate's success story in dial-up was not long-lived. While consumer preferences for national plans doomed Megagate in the cellular market, here the culprit was the expanding fiber networks that allowed customers to access broadband Internet. "We still have some dial-up customers. It's folks who live in rural areas and don't really have an option," Kevin told us.

So again, Megagate found itself having to reinvent. Seeing gaps in the services provided by the Big Boys to local businesses, Kevin led Megagate into this segment.

"Probably the biggest value proposition you get with Megagate is 'This is our garden.' Hattiesburg is not on most people's map. It's the corner of most people's garden, and the water doesn't always reach to the corner. We water our garden really well. If one of our customers has AT&T, he'd be lucky to get the same person—or *a* person—on a phone call. He wouldn't have the president of the company pop in to see how things are going. If I go to see a customer, I tour their business. I have a better idea of what we need to be doing to serve him. We know all of our customers, and we're very helpful. I get on our engineers because I don't think we bill enough for things we do."

Like Mike Bodart at Hoosier Sporting Goods or Dave Bobbitt at Community 1st Bank, Kevin Pack and Megagate have built strategy around service and strong relationships with clients. Building these ties to customers is labor intensive and expensive—but it's also a difficult capability for large companies to match. Large companies have advantages too, however, and the changing weather of these markets often arises from the scale-related cost advantage of larger companies in relation to the service advantage of smaller ones.

And just as the big cellular carriers moved in on Megagate, large phone and Internet providers are now encroaching on the company's market. "Comcast beats us on price," Kevin admitted. "They moved into our market about two years ago, selling phone and Internet. They've had a lot of success in the smaller business market, which is largely what we have around here."

Reinventing yet again, Megagate is now taking advantage of technical advances to carry voice and data to customers' buildings wirelessly. This operational change required significant personnel changes and capital investments. "Within the last year, we hired back one of our old employees who had gone to work for Alltel and Verizon. He's a wireless guy at heart. We found that we can use a wireless shot to replace the loops and, in some cases, fiber optics lines that we have to pay a monthly lease on. You probably did not notice that we have a forty-foot wireless tower on top of the building."

We hadn't, but if we had, we would have worried that the storm was going to blow the tower down onto us.

Kevin knows that the strategy he's developed for wireless is just another temporary solution until the next technological sea change, but he also knows he can look only so far ahead. "In the next year or two, we're building wireless networks. Is that going to take us where we need to go long-term? I don't know. I certainly feel good about what it's going to do for us for a couple of years. But because of technological issues, regulatory issues, and competitive issues, I don't know where it's going."

Kevin's understanding of the third corollary to Mazzeo's Law—and his constant search for a match between changing market needs and his company's capabilities—are what gives Megagate a fighting chance to stay relevant in this fast-moving business.

And this brings us to the end of the road, so to speak. We have spent much of this book sharing lessons with you, and so it seems fitting to end with some lessons *we* learned over the course of the Roadside MBA project.

We learned that the small business owners of America are incredibly passionate, hardworking, and intelligent. We saw so much to admire. We also found that while being single can be fun, it gets old pretty quick. Surprisingly, perhaps, we each settled into happy long-term relationships over the course of this project.

We affirmed that our ivory tower strategy frameworks are real; the economic forces that shape business strategy were evident on every single day of our travels. We also learned a lot about each other, and we regretted, at times, that it is not possible to unlearn things.

And we observed that getting strategy right requires constant problem-solving and tireless determination to unpack the "it depends" of good business decision-making. Mazzeo's Law is why, we think, the profession of management is so difficult, so challenging, but also so much fun.

We're excited to keep learning and keep traveling. After all, Mike and Scott have some work to do to catch up with Paul, who has now been to all fifty states. So join us soon for *Roadside MBA, North Dakota and Alaska Edition*.

Businesses Visited

Jonesboro, Arkansas:
BRACES BY BURRIS

Denver, North Carolina:
STEELE RUBBER
PRODUCTS, INC.

Gresham, Oregon:
SILK ESPRESSO

Hattiesburg, Mississippi:
MUGSHOTS GRILL
AND BAR

Jonesboro, Arkansas:
WILCOXSON'S KIDS
PLACE

Dothan, Alabama:
KEY FIRE HOSE

Marietta, Georgia:
PRODEW INC.

Pensacola, Florida:
COLLEGEFROG

Frankfort, Kentucky:
FIT TIME FOR
WOMEN

Missoula, Montana:
BANK OF MONTANA

Post Falls, Idaho:
COMMUNITY 1ST
BANK

Pasco, Washington:
TILITE

Council Bluffs, Iowa:
ARNOLD TOOL

Marietta, Georgia:
MARIETTA NDT

Smyrna, Georgia:
DOGMA DOG CARE

Hattiesburg, Mississippi:
MISSISSIPPI MUSIC

Hickory, North Carolina:
BLIND SQUIRREL
DIGITAL

Johnson City, Tennessee:
MORRIS-BAKER
FUNERAL HOME AND
CREMATION
SERVICES

Liberal, Kansas:
COLLINS DIAMONDS

Spartanburg, South
Carolina:
PRICES' STORE FOR
MEN

Hickory, North Carolina:
CLATER KAYE
THEATREWORKS

Missoula, Montana:
EKO COMPOST

Jefferson City, Missouri:
WREN SOLUTIONS

Slidell, Louisiana:
GAYLORD CHEMICAL

Dothan, Alabama:
PANHANDLE
CONVERTER
RECYCLING

Enid, Oklahoma:
PT COUPLING

Saint Joseph, Missouri:
SOUTHSIDE FAMILY
FUN CENTER

Pensacola, Florida:
RE VERA SERVICES

Enid, Oklahoma:
AEROSOCK

Saint Joseph, Missouri:
SAINT JOE
DISTRIBUTING

Johnson City, Tennessee:
EAGLE'S LANDING
INFORMATICS

Coeur d'Alene, Idaho:
KLEIN'S DKI

Saint Joseph, Missouri:
JR'S TBA

Cincinnati, Ohio:
PLASTIC MOLDINGS
COMPANY

Council Bluffs, Iowa:
STUART TINLEY LAW
FIRM

Jefferson City, Missouri:
MIDWEST PRODUCTS
GROUP

Athol, Idaho:
SILVERWOOD THEME
PARK

Middletown, Ohio:
BERNS GARDEN
CENTER

Richland, Washington:
ELEVATE

Reno, Nevada:
SUNDANCE BOOKS
AND MUSIC

Pueblo, Colorado:
GPS SOURCE

Spartanburg, South
Carolina:
LAUNCH SOMETHING

Bloomington, Illinois:
PRENZLER OUTDOOR
ADVERTISING

Columbus, Indiana:
HOOSIER SPORTING
GOODS

Hattiesburg, Mississippi:
MEGAGATE

Acknowledgments

We are grateful to all the small business owners who met with us over the last few years. We were amazed at how many people were willing to take time out of their busy schedules to sit down and tell us their stories. The demands of their businesses were large, and the old adage "time is money" applied perfectly. There would be no *Roadside MBA* without their generosity.

Representatives of local Chambers of Commerce were often helpful in setting up visits. Shaun Sappenfield (Jefferson City), Matt Parker (Dothan), and Kelly Reeser (Pensacola) went above and beyond, and we appreciate their time and energy.

Our agent, Zoë Pagnamenta, was immediately enthusiastic about this project. We are grateful for her help refining the general idea of the book, her input on who might read it, and her comments on various drafts.

The input of our editor at Grand Central Publishing, John Brodie, was critical. John was always available to offer knowledge of the market or to settle the occasional co-author fight. He shared our vision of what the project was about, so much so that we thought it would be fun to let him tag along on a trip. Unfortunately, John is a city boy and would get nervous if he could not simply hail a cab to get to his next appointment.

We are very grateful to Daniel Zox, who provided technical support and made a promotional video after taking footage of our travels in Dothan. He also read and commented on previous drafts, as did Andrea Miller, Cheryl Miller, Ryan McDevitt, and many students.

Mike: I would like to thank my dissertation adviser, Tim Bresnahan, who taught me that economics is about real people making real decisions and showed me that small towns are a good place to look for economic insights.

I am very lucky to be working at Kellogg, where I am enriched by my colleagues and my students. That's also where I met Scott and Paul, who I thank for helping me to get hired at Kellogg in the first place and for including me on this adventure.

My mother, Rita Mazzeo, provided inspiration to me in finishing this project. Finally, I thank Daniel Zox for being a constant source of support and kindness.

Paul: I am incredibly lucky to work at the Stanford Graduate School of Business. The input of my colleagues, the support of the administration, and the discussions in class all make me a much better economist than I would otherwise be and make coming to "work" a joy.

Kathryn Stoner is the best thing to happen to me during this book project. I thank her for her constant encouragement, positive outlook, and endless humor. I hope she reads this, though she may hold out for *Roadside MBA, Canada Edition*.

Scott and Mike were great to work with when we were all together at Kellogg. It's been my pleasure to have a chance to work with them so intimately once again. I learn a lot from them every day (but please don't tell them I said that).

Scott: I'm grateful to my employer, the David Eccles School of Business at the University of Utah. I'd also like to thank the students and faculty at the Jon M. Huntsman School of Business at Utah State University and the Kellogg School of Management at Northwestern University for welcoming me as a visiting professor during the completion of this book. At these institutions, Taylor Randall, Bill Hesterly, Doug Anderson, and Tom Hubbard merit special mention.

On the home front, my parents, Joe and Coke Schaefer, provide far more support than a grown son ought to need. Shelly Jones remains the World's Best Nanny. Andrea Miller single-handedly makes Salt Lake City a place to call home.

Finally, I'm grateful to Mike and Paul. Despite what you may have read, they're really not so bad to travel with.

Index

Index 277